PRAYER PRIMER

God bless
you!

Fr. Bill Schott

THOMAS DUBAY, S.M.

PRAYER PRIMER

Igniting a Fire Within

PUBLISHED BY ST. ANTHONY MESSENGER PRESS
CINCINNATI, OHIO

Cover art:
Alessandro Allori
Christ in the House of Mary and Martha
Erich Lessing/Art Resource, N.Y.

Cover by Riz Boncan Marsella

Library of Congress Cataloging-in-Publication Data

Dubay, Thomas.
   Prayer primer : igniting a fire within / by Thomas Dubay.
         p. cm.
Includes index.
   ISBN 1-56955-339-4 (alk. paper)
   I. Prayer—Catholic Church. I. Title.
   BV215 .D82 2002
   248.3′2—dc21

                                        2002000008

ISBN-13: 978-1-56955-339-8
ISBN-10: 1-56955-339-4
Library of Congress Control Number 2002000008
Copyright © 2002 Ignatius Press, San Francisco. All rights reserved.

Published by Servant Books, an imprint of
St. Anthony Messenger Press
28 W. Liberty St.
Cincinnati, OH 45202
www.AmericanCatholic.org
www.ServantBooks.org

Printed in the United States of America
Printed on acid-free paper

10 11 12 13 14   9 8 7 6 5

CONTENTS

III

CHURCH AND FAMILY

IV

QUESTIONS AND PROBLEMS

PREFACE

In the important matters of human life beginners need help: learning, thinking, reading, writing, relating with others.

The most momentous of all human activities, relating with God, is no exception. *Prayer Primer* is intended to aid beginners in prayer. We especially envision people who somehow sense that communion with God should have at least a significant place in their lives, and yet they are not quite sure what prayer is or how to go about it. Many want to grow in their prayer lives but are not at all confident as to just what that would entail.

In these pages I shall try to combine clarity and simplicity with respect for the intelligence of the reader. I ask that no one interpret "beginner" in these pages to be equivalent to uneducated. A person can have a doctorate in one field and be a novice in another. While we shall avoid complex academic language, our text will call for reflective pondering on the part of young and old alike, and of everyone in their middle years as well. Our subject is both simple and deep.

I should like to take occasion here to thank Brother Sean Wright, O.Ss.S for his highly competent reading and critiquing of the text. He has provided a signal service to both the author and the reader.

ABBREVIATIONS

CCC   *Catechism of the Catholic Church*

CD   *Christus Dominus*, Vatican Council II, Decree on the Pastoral Office of Bishops

EPB   *Evidential Power of Beauty*, Thomas Dubay, S.M.

FW   *Fire Within*, Thomas Dubay, S.M.

GILH   *General Instruction of the Liturgy of the Hours*, Sacred Congregation for Divine Worship

JB   *Jerusalem Bible*

LC   *Laudis Canticum*, Paul VI, promulgation of the new Liturgy of the Hours

LG   *Lumen gentium*, Vatican Council II, Constitution on the Church

OT   *Optatam totius*, Vatican Council II, Decree on Priestly Training

SC   *Sacrosanctum concilium*, Vatican Council II, Constitution on the Liturgy

SSD   *Seeking Spiritual Direction*, Thomas Dubay, S.M.

PART ONE

PRELIMINARIES

I

Thirsting and Quenching

Men and women everywhere are hungry and thirsty, voraciously yearning and seeking: rich and poor, wise and foolish, young and old, literate and illiterate, saints and sinners, atheists and agnostics, playboys and prostitutes. Some can explain their inner emptiness in words; most cannot, but everyone experiences it. That inner ache drives all our dreams, desires, and decisions—good and bad. Even your decision to pick up this book and read was triggered by this nameless desire.

Our abiding hunger for more than we presently experience does not have to be proved but only explained. Which is what we propose to do right now, before we even begin to think about what prayer is all about. Otherwise you and I cannot understand fully the splendid reality of communing deeply with our Creator and Lord and of our unspeakable destiny in and with him.

Mere animals do not and cannot have this inner aching need, for the simple reason that material things are satisfied with visible creation and their place in it. Because you and I have intellects and wills rooted in our profound spiritual core, nothing finite and limited does, or ever can, fill us. Deep in our humanness is an ache for fullness, for infinity. We are completely satisfied by no individual egoism, by no series of selfish pursuits: vanity, fame, money, lust, power, drugs. Always the sinner seeks more accolades, more money, more recognition, more lewd eroticism, more control of others, more drugs. Never is he satisfied, never really happy and fulfilled.

Why is this so? As spirit-in-the-flesh beings, you and I burst beyond the material order, beyond what our senses can attain, beyond the cosmos itself. By its limited nature nothing created can satisfy us. God alone, the sole infinite One, can fill our endless yearnings. As Karl Rahner put it, we are oriented by nature to the Absolute. Or as John Courtney Murray expressed it, the problem now is not how to be a man, but how to become more than a man. Or as St. Augustine put it in his classic prayer: "You have made us for yourself, O Lord, and our hearts are restless until they rest in you." Kittens and giraffes do not have this problem. They cannot. You and I do. (See CCC 27–30.)

Quenching and prayer

What does this have to do with a primer on prayer? Much, very much. Prayer is not merely a pious reaction to suffering or a means to get us out of trouble. We are the only beings in visible creation who cannot attain fulfillment without becoming more than we are, therefore without the divine. Ducks and camels, trees and stars need matter alone. In other words, you and I are transcendent beings whose needs go beyond this universe. That is why our destiny must be God and no one else. That is why prayer is absolutely basic. This is the divine plan, and no other plan comes close. At the heart of our human reality there must be a relationship and communion with the divine. Otherwise we simply do not make it; we do not and cannot flourish and attain our destiny. (See EPB, pp. 17–20.)

Prayer, therefore, is both simple and deep—and, as we shall see later on, immensely enriching, leading to unspeakable love and delight. Prayer is not complicated, because there is nothing more natural than to converse with your beloved, and most especially with your supreme Beloved. If all grows normally it becomes deep, because, as we have explained, it is rooted in your profound human and spiritual reality, in who and what you are as a man or a woman.

The illness of boredom

But we need to look at all this from another point of view, the downside of our human situation. Among the saddest pictures we meet in life is a jaded face: the visage of one who "has done it all", whose life through wanton sin is a shambles. It is a countenance that expresses no joy, no peace, no excitement, no enthusiasm, no interest, no hope, no love, no fulfillment. Behind that face is an inner desert of degenerate exhaustion, completely empty of lively delight.

Jadedness is extreme boredom, but there are lesser degrees, of course. But even lesser shadings are abnormalities. Human beings are meant to be alive and vibrant, full of wonder, love, and happiness—which is exactly what Scripture promises to those who embrace God's word fully. This is what the saints experience, what people who have a deep prayer life know to be the case. They "rejoice in the Lord always", not just some of the time (Phil 4:4).

Jadedness and boredom and an absence of vibrant prayer comprise one reason among others that the great novelist Fyodor Dostoyevsky was right on target when he made the comment that "to live without God is nothing but torture." Not everyone admits this, of course. One reason is pathological denial. Another is that when people are so submerged in self-centered pleasure seeking, they cannot see what some silence and solitude and honesty would make obvious to them. A third explanation for the denial is that bored people often use pleasures, both licit and illicit, as so many narcotics that tend to dull the deep inner pain of their emptiness. This human aching is always lurking in the center of their being, but it is faced only in honest silence. The print and electronic media offer endless proof day after day that Dostoevsky was right, but few care to see and to listen. Facing reality as it is requires honesty. As Jesus himself put it: We cannot serve both God and mammon (Mt 6:24). If it is not the first, it will be the second. Nature abhors a vacuum.

This famous novelist went on to remark that atheists should actually be called idolators. Why? When one rejects the real God, he inevitably substitutes lesser things to fill his inner emptiness. Everyone, we should notice, has one or more consuming interests that occupy his desires and dreams. If we are not captivated by the living God and pursuing him, we will center our desires on idols, big or small: vanities, pleasure seeking, prestige, power, and others we have already noted. While the idols never satisfy, they often do serve as narcotics that more or less deaden the inner pain of not having him for whom we were made and who alone can bring us to the eternal ecstasy of the beatific vision.

Yes, if you and I are not seriously pursuing the real God, inevitably we will focus on things that can never satisfy us. We are chasing after dead ends. Prayer is the path to reality/Reality.

Quenching at the fountain

Scripture says it best of all. With a charming invitation the Lord shouts "Oh, come to the water all you who are thirsty; though you have no money, come. . . . Why spend money on what is not bread, your wages on what fails to satisfy. . . . Pay attention, come to me; listen, and your soul will live" (Is 55:1–3, JB). Nothing less can bring us to life. And Isaiah himself keeps vigil through the night as his spirit yearns for his Lord (Is 26:9). He practices what he proclaims.

The psalmist is of like mind: his soul thirsts for the living God (Ps 42:2–3). Like a parched desert he pines for his Lord, for only in him does he find rest (Ps 63:1; 62:1). The inspired writer knows that God must be our consuming concern, for pursuing him, adoring him, loving him, being immersed in him can alone profoundly delight and fill us. Anything less than Everything is not enough.

The New Testament has the same message, for the

Fountain has appeared in the flesh. He declares in the Sermon on the Mount that they are blessed who hunger and thirst after holiness (Mt 5:6), and his Mother proclaims in her Magnificat that the Lord fills the hungry with every good thing (Lk 1:53). Jesus explicitly invites all those who are thirsty to come to him for a quenching with living water (Jn 7:37). At the very end of both Testaments this same invitation is extended to everyone: let all the thirsty come forward to be forever quenched with the life-giving waters, that is, an eternal enthrallment in Father, Son, and Holy Spirit seen face to face (Rev 22:17).

Prayer life is therefore profoundly rooted in the needs of our human nature. Without it we are frustrated creatures. All the way from the beginnings in vocal prayer through meditation, which leads to the summit of contemplation, this prayerful immersion in the indwelling Trinity gradually transforms us from one glory to another as we are being turned into the divine image (2 Cor 3:18). Here alone do men and women become "perfect in beauty" (Ezek 16:13–14). We can understand why Henri de Lubac was prompted to say that man is truly man only when the light of God is reflected in a face upturned in prayer.

2

Another Book on Prayer?

Given the thousands of religiously oriented books that are published each decade, those dealing with prayer seem to be among the most popular. Happily, disillusionment with the superficial glitter of materialism and its unfulfilled promises is settling upon many thoughtful people today. Turning to the only realistic alternative, God himself, obviously brings up the question of prayer, making contact with him.

Yet, it would seem at first glance that little or nothing new remains to be said about this subject. Why more books and articles? Why this one in particular? One reason is that while basic truths do not change, times and people do. There is no doubt that God is touching more than a few people in our day, some of them deeply indeed. They are hungry for God, but do not know just where or how to start responding. Because all of us are citizens of this twenty-first century, we ask our questions and face our needs in our context, not in that of a previous age.

A second reason for this volume is that many of the topics and themes we shall discuss are seldom spoken or

written about for ordinary people, that is, without schol-
arly detail and many footnotes. While we shall assume
that readers of this little work are intelligent, we shall
not presuppose that they need or have a theological back-
ground. Prayer is simple and uncomplicated, even though
it normally becomes profound and rich—if all goes normally.

Chapter 1 may serve as an illustration of our first two
reasons. While the theme of thirsting for God is prominent in Scripture, and should be in any age, seeing prayer,
especially deepening prayer, as rooted in an inner hunger
is not sufficiently accented today. Chapter 3 will explore
further ramifications of this fundamental reality.

A third reason for this primer is the sad fact that some
current ideas need to be countered. A correspondent recently wrote to me that "we have all sorts of nonsense
to unlearn. I vividly remember the course in meditation
when I was taking my theology degree at ———— College.
There was no mention of virtue, conversion, or anything
of the sort—but we were reminded that we should be
barefoot for meditation, since energies come in through
the feet."

The final answer to our query, "Why this book?" is
that we shall be answering questions our contemporaries
are asking. Let me mention a sampling of them—there
are many others.

Practical questions

Just what is prayer all about? Are there many kinds of
prayer? How much time should I give to prayer in my

typical day? Where is the best place to pray? What can I do about distractions? What should I think and do about feeling dry and empty and not inclined to pray at all? How do I get started in living a more serious prayer life?

What is the place of vocal prayers in our lives? Should we make up our own prayers or use those found in books and pamphlets? Can a person be saying too many vocal prayers? Are vocal prayers (morning and evening, rosary, way of the cross, litanies, and so on) enough, or should I be thinking also of meditation and contemplation? If so, how do they fit together?

Then there are questions about prayer in marriage and family life. Is a regular and serious growth in prayer possible in marriage? If so, how is this achieved? For example, how can husbands and wives today find the prayerful solitude Jesus lived and taught? Are they, too, called to meditative and contemplative prayer and its summit? How do they find the time needed? How do married saints handle these questions? Is the Liturgy of the Hours meant for lay people as well as for priests and religious? How do parents explain and teach prayer to their children?

What is Christocentric meditation, and how does it differ from an oriental awareness and techniques? Are New Age ideas worth looking into? What should we think of centering prayer? What do you think of the charismatic renewal? What is Christocentric contemplation? Is that the same as "deep prayer"? Does Scripture speak much about meditation and contemplation? How do they differ? What do Vatican Council II and the *Catechism of the Catholic Church* say about them? When and how does one

begin to meditate . . . and then later on commence contemplation?

To find quick answers to these and many other questions consult the index at the back of this volume. But
for the best overall understanding and enlightenment, you
will want to read and ponder each of the chapters, one
by one. You may need to read some of them more than
once. Yes, and think. They are brief; the task is not huge.
The rewards are great.

Bon voyage!

3

Why Pray?

If a roving reporter were to take a random sample of a hundred of our fellow citizens at church services on Sunday morning and pose to them the title question of this chapter, it is a safe guess that the majority, perhaps a large majority, would describe prayer in terms of seeking divine help in solving problems of one kind or another: illness, employment, fear, guilt feelings, interpersonal conflicts. As the saying goes, there are no atheists in foxholes. This reason for praying is valid, but by itself it is notably incomplete.

If five different people pick up this book, or fall on their knees at the end of a long day, they may easily be prompted by five specifically different motives. One may be suffering and wants to find a way to cope. A second may have had a run-in with husband or wife and is hurting inside. A third is perhaps responding to an inner emptiness. A fourth is simply doing what was learned at Mom's knees. The fifth is deeply in love with God and cannot imagine beginning or ending a day without adoring and praising him—and thus loving him more and more. To put this last motivation in contemporary terms, this man or woman is beginning to fall in love and thus perceives that prayer is interpersonal contact, relationship, union, intimacy. Our motivation picture is now getting more complete.

Seeing the big picture

Yet more needs to be said: namely, seeing prayer in perspective. Among the astonishing realities in this enormous universe in which we humans are working out our eternal destiny, not simply providing for the next few decades, is the fact that the visible and invisible aspects of reality are in communication with each other. You and I as incarnated spirits (both material and spiritual in our makeup) are alone sharers in both elements. We experience both matter and spirit.

Albert Einstein marveled that atoms, molecules, cells, galaxies are comprehensible, that is, that they can be understood by our finite human minds. Astonishing it is that our mathematical formulas, equations, and laws so precisely describe visible reality as it actually is and operates. Still more surprising is the love affair the Lord of the galaxies wishes to have with men and women dwelling on a particular planet circling an ordinary (yet amazing) star we call the sun. This one star is almost a million miles in diameter, an enormously raging nuclear inferno, and yet it is only one among billions of other stars in this Milky Way galaxy of ours. And our galaxy is only one of up to a hundred billion comparable galaxies. On the tiny planet you and I inhabit, the love communication to which the divine Artist invites us dwarfs anything science and technology can imagine or foresee. By comparison the Internet and cyberspace are paltry. The names of this inexpressible love affair are revelation and prayer, two gratuitous gifts that no one has the least right to claim.

So why do we pray?

Most people would consider a five-minute chat with a famous person, or even a brief letter, to be an undeserved favor. They could not forget the former and probably would save the latter. Never would their reaction be a blank silence. Prayer is a precious privilege—and this is putting it mildly. That the Lord of glory, himself unending joy, beauty, and goodness, would invite us to communicate with him and then begin the conversation with his inspired word, which welcomes our responses, is an unimaginable blessing. It ought not to surprise us that the psalmist's heart and flesh tingle for very joy at this prospect. He has tasted the incomparable goodness and beauty of his God (Ps 84:2; 34:8).

A second reason for prayer is what we may call virtue needs. If noble people feel an inner necessity to thank a stranger for holding the door open, surely we should feel the need to thank our Origin and our Destiny profusely "always and everywhere" (Eph 5:20, JB), not only for our very existence but for our every breath, not to mention endless other favors. So also we need to express sorrow for our sins and ask the grace to overcome them, to shout praise to the glory of our God in his awesome economy of salvation, to sing to the beauty of creation and its Creator. At other times we need to cry out to him in our pain and sufferings, or to yearn for him to fill our inner emptiness, or to experience a wordless absorption in his divine beauty.

A third way of expressing why we pray is to say that we cannot achieve our human fulfillment without communing with God—and the deeper our prayer, the deeper our fulfillment. As Scripture puts it, we become "perfect in beauty" because of the divine splendor that is given in a profound communion with the Lord (Ezek 16:13–14). In the very heights of contemplative prayer heroic virtue is given. One becomes (as St. John of the Cross notes) awesomely strong. This is the reason saints possess a miraculous goodness, a level of living neither they nor we can attain of ourselves. (See FW, pp. 3–4; 184–85; 209–10.)

Not surprisingly, this leads to our next motive for prayer: we bond with others more readily and are good for them to the precise degree of our immersion in God who is love. Husbands and wives have a beneficial impact on each other and on their children to the extent that they are growing in all the virtues—which is to say to the extent of their prayer depth. Their influence is deeper and eternal. The same is true of the priest at the bedside or in the confessional or in the pulpit.

This is why saints in any state in life do immeasurably more to benefit others than mediocre people do. Prayer triggers a snowball effect in the good we do to others. Hence, a husband who really loves his wife and children will take pains to become a man of deep prayer. So also will the wife and mother—and the teacher, doctor, priest, religious, everyone. It is easy to say, "I love you", but not easy to prove it. Saints love their spouses and children, their students and parishioners and patients, far, far more than the lukewarm do. Authenticity works.

Examples furnish us with a cluster of reasons for growing in a serious prayer life. Prime among them, of course, is Jesus himself. The Gospels tell us a number of times how he would get up "long before dawn" and go off where he could be alone to be absorbed in prayerful solitude with the Father (Mk 1:35). He even spent the whole night in prayer before he selected his twelve apostles (Lk 6:12). We are told that these times of long, prayerful solitude were habitual with him (Lk 5:16; see also Mk 6:46; Lk 9:18, 28; 21:37). He had to instruct overbusy Martha that her sister Mary, in her contemplative decision to set everything else aside to give undivided attention to Jesus' person and words, had "chosen the better part" and that "it would not be taken from her" (Lk 10:38–42). In other words, Mary was beginning in dark faith the eternal contemplative enthrallment of immersion in the trinitarian beauty seen face to face.

The saints universally imitate their Master in making continual union with the Father to be "the one thing", the top priority in their lives. They have learned that Jesus in the Martha-Mary account was referring to Psalm 27:4, which had declared that "gazing on the beauty of the LORD" is the overriding necessity in everyone's hierarchy of importances.

If anyone on our planet were to have a reason to relegate prayer to a secondary place in his daily round of duties, one might think it to be the man who has six billion people to be concerned about. It is difficult to grasp how one individual could have packed into a single lifetime the almost incredible list of accomplishments of which we read in the life of Pope John Paul II. Yet he remarked one day that "the pope's first duty is prayer." A salutary homily for the lesser of us.

4

Getting the Feel

Most people, it would seem, think of prayer as vocal expression, especially in asking God for what we need, and indeed thus it is. Vocal prayer is so important that we shall devote an entire chapter to it, and two other chapters to liturgical prayer. Jesus himself admonishes us to ask, seek, and knock. Yet at the same time prayer is lots else too. We have already noted that the psalmist declares that immersing ourselves in the divine loveliness, that is, contemplation, is the most important of our daily privileges and duties. This love-penetrated union with the indwelling Father, Son, and Holy Spirit entails a personal "transformation from one glory to another" into the very divine image itself (2 Cor 3:18). Any serious theist can see that this has to be the overriding necessity in any human life.

Interpersonal intimacy

In our contemporary media the word "intimacy" usually refers to sexual relations. In the mutual self-gift of a committed marriage open to new life this usage is correct. But egocentric carnal contacts are quite the opposite of interpersonal. Mere animals engage in them, and there is by definition nothing interpersonal involved. Sin is always self-centered, even when accompanied by amorous expressions. Lust is exploitation.

Intimacy is by no means first of all physical closeness. Two bricks cemented to each other are not models of intimacy. People who will and do good to others, even when nothing is received in return, are the ones who love genuinely. They are personally close precisely to the degree that they are devoted to the other's welfare and advantage.

There are of course degrees of union and intimacy with the Lord. In all of them God speaks first, not usually in audible, human words, but in a divine manner. He gives us the very inclination and desire to turn to him with our needs and also our will to adore and love (1 Jn 4:19). We on our part need to be alert to and listen for his message and light, as did the boy Samuel: "Speak LORD, for your servant is listening" (1 Sam 3:9–10). At the beginning of this relationship one speaks to God with words, either one's own or from a set formula. And just as in ordinary human relationships this intimacy grows to the extent that we live the gospel generously—which, naturally enough, includes giving adequate time to prayer itself.

Amazingly, God deeply desires this communion with us. He thirsts for us, not because he needs us, but because he is pure love. "Whether we realize it or not, prayer is the encounter of God's thirst with ours. God thirsts that we may thirst for him" (CCC 2560: a thought borrowed from St. Augustine; for prayer as relationship with God, see CCC 2558–65).

Of all interpersonal intimacies open to the human person contemplative prayer in its advanced stages of development is incomparably the greatest. Mystics, the men and women of profoundest immersion in the indwelling Trinity, are unanimous in declaring that these depths immeasurably surpass any other experience. They are literally unspeakable. St. Paul is of a like mind when he tells the Corinthians that the human eye has not seen, nor ear heard, nor can the human mind even imagine what splendors God has prepared for those who love him (1 Cor 2:9). Worldly people are little inclined to suspect or believe all this, but we should not be surprised—they have no experience of the reality. They are like a man born blind challenging the description of a magnificent painting.

Communing in mystery

Everything in visible creation from the tiny atom to immense galaxies is mysterious (a mixture of knowing and unknowing), even to the expert, and especially to the expert. The one who knows much about anything knows far better than the uneducated how much he does not know about it. Despite the wonders our various sciences daily uncover, we always find new marvels and questions and mysteries. Our human knowledge is necessarily a mingling of positive knowing together with a cut-off of knowing: we grasp only so much and no more at any given time. This is why nothing is completely clear and fully known to us. We do not even know ourselves with complete lucidity. Because God is endless power, light, beauty, and love, with no limit whatsoever, he must be the deepest of mysteries. If this were not so, he would not be God.

Consequently getting closer to him on earth must absolutely be shrouded in darkness. It could not be otherwise. We know him, but never fully. Even the summit of contemplative prayer is attained in darkness, for in this life no one can see God (Jn 1:18). Only in the ecstasy of the beatific vision, when we shall behold the unsurpassable beauty of Father, Son, and Holy Spirit face to face, shall our contemplation be perfectly clear. Through the empowerment of the light of glory we shall drink infinite Splendor in unclouded and unending glory.

Paradoxically the selfish shall be empty, whereas the selfless shall be filled. The sinner scrambles to achieve satiety, but he ends up gulping air. The saint in giving up all self-centered clinging attains the Lord of the universe and all else with him. In this as in all else, the first shall be last, and the last shall be first. It is, after all, by the hard road and the narrow gate that we find fullest living and the most genuine joy (Mt 7:13-14).

In sincere prayer we turn our puny selves to the supreme Other. Even though growth is a gradual process, when we break free of egocentrism we find abiding delight. "He fills the hungry with good things", says the Mother of Jesus. Indeed he does. As prayer deepens a point can be reached where a person becomes so absorbed in triune Beauty that he is conscious of the Beloved alone. There is no other love like it on our planet—which raises our next point.

The aim: To fall in love

One of the beauties of divine revelation is that everything is summed up in one reality: love. God is (not simply, has) purest, unending love (1 Jn 4:8), and whatever good we happen to be doing, if it is done well, is living love in action (2 Jn 6). Because truth is symphonic—it makes one concert of beauty—it follows that the aim of all prayer is eventually to be head over heels in love with Love, Father, Son, and Holy Spirit. When that happens we are then going to love everyone, even our enemies and those who neglect us.

The answer to our question of getting a feel for what prayer essentially is—all types of prayer—we find splendidly etched by St. Paul: As we get closer and closer to God, we are transformed from one glory to another, and we thus become more and more like the One we love (2 Cor 3:18). Everything we have said thus far, and shall say to the last sentence of this book, is summarized in this one idea.

All this may strike some people as utopian and merely romantic. If so, I would suggest that they set aside the glitter and superficiality of the entertainment industry for a few hours a day for a week and ponder what we have been saying. They will find that, yes, we have traced an outline of the supreme romance. And it has the advantage of being true.

5

Elegant Variety

Now that we have the feel for prayer as an interpersonal contact/union of slowly developing intimacy between the indwelling Trinity and the human person, we are prepared to appreciate the rich variations in which this relationship occurs. There is no written explanation of this wealth comparable to finding it on the lips of the Lord in his inspired word.

As we have noted, many people think of prayer mainly as asking for help in our sundry problems and needs. Fewer still think of it as being in love with God and expressing that love in many diverse ways, often in touching and tender terms. But such is the scriptural reality. In order to handle clearly this extraordinary abundance of interpersonal beauty, I think it best to sample these biblical prayer themes under several headings. Your own use of the Bible and participation in the eucharistic liturgy will furnish you with many more examples of these themes.

1. *Petitionary prayer.* We begin with a type of prayer that is familiar to everyone—even to the former atheist in the

foxhole. We are to ask and it will be given to us, seek and we shall find, knock and the door will be opened (Mt 7:7–8). We are to call on this God who works wonders for those he loves (see Ps 4:3, JB). Just as infants turn with complete trust to their parents for all of their needs, so we also cast our cares on the Lord, because he cares for us tenderly beyond our imagining (1 Pet 5:7).

2. *Adoration, praise, blessing.* Filled with joy, we worship our Origin and our final Destiny, purest goodness and beauty (Ps 16:5–11). We join with "everything that lives and breathes" in a hymn of praise (Ps 150:6; 96:1–2; 98:4–8). We bless and praise this God, not simply once in a while, but at all times (Ps 34:1). We glorify him as the worker of marvels on our behalf (Ps 31:21), as we celebrate his everlasting love in outpourings of tribute and thanksgiving (Ps 136:1–26). All this occurs in an atmosphere of blessing and rejoicing in the tender love of the Creator toward everything he has made (cf. Ps 146:1–2; 150:1–6).

3. *Thanksgiving.* Closely akin to adoration and praise, and yet with an added dimension, is heartfelt thanksgiving. Repeatedly the psalmist and the Church hearken to our privilege and duty of expressing gratitude to the Father for every good and perfect gift that descends from him (Jas 1:17). All of us are to declare to this God an endless proclamation of thanksgiving (cf. Ps 28:7; Col 3:15).

4. *Longing and yearning.* In its advancing stages the pursuit of God includes a hungering and thirsting for him

as though we were a parched desert in need of a soaking rain, or as a doe longs for the running waters of a stream (Ps 63:1; 42:1–2). At times in life we need quietly and patiently to wait for the Lord, who will fill us in due time (Ps 37:7; 40:1). The psalmist seeks to understand better, to celebrate, to love, and to observe the precepts and plans of the Lord (Ps 119:1–176).

5. *Prayerful suffering.* Since all of us suffer in one way or another, and in diverse degrees, it is not surprising that the biblical word would teach us how to bear our crosses in life and how to use them to come to a closer communion with the indwelling Trinity. Jesus, of course, leads the way: in the midst of his agony in the garden of olives he shares with the Father his inner pains and expresses his desire that the divine will be done (Mt 26:39). We, too, express our heartaches to this same loving Father and unload our burdens before him (Ps 55:4–5, 16–17, 22; 62:8). We may even cry out in our pains and sufferings (Ps 22; 23:4–6; 27:7).

6. *Sorrowing for sin.* There is need in any honest heart to join David and the publican in begging pardon of the all-holy God, for we are sinners (many psalms; Lk 18:13). The first step in obtaining forgiveness is to confess humbly that we have sinned. Then we renounce the sin, express sorrow, and return to the Father, firmly resolved to profit from our experience and to be deeply converted (Ps 32:1–5; 51; Lk 15:11–24). Since serious sin wounds the sinner profoundly and issues in bitter guilt, he wisely returns to the only one who can heal him

fully, and he seeks relief from the divine forgiving love (Ps 38:1–10, 17–18, 21–22).

7. *Marveling and wondering at the divine works.* The psalmist, being vibrantly alive as a person, is alert to and therefore aware of the marvels God works both in creation and in salvation history (Ps 96; 104; 135; 107; 139:1–18). The prayerful person not only notices these astonishing things the Lord has done in his world, he ponders them, fixes them in his memory (Ps 46:8). Furthermore, he celebrates the glories of creation and finds great joy in the divine Artist and his splendors (Ps 104:1–35; 111:2–3). We should notice that to celebrate is to affirm the goodness and beauty of a thing or person or event. On Independence Day we proclaim the blessings of living in a free country. To celebrate a person's birthday is to declare in words and action that this person's existence is a gift. Celebrating is singing to existence, a yes-ing of reality, exulting in the real—either with words or without them. The psalter is full of examples . . . and so also are they found in the minds and on the lips of the saints.

8. *Meditation.* It is not accidental that the first two verses of the inspired book of prayer deal with discursive meditation, that is, with thinking over and applying the word of God to one's life, and then in inwardly communing with him about it. Happy is that man who receives this word and then reflects on it in his heart day and night (Ps 1:1–2). Joshua is likewise to ponder the law of the Lord day and night (Josh 1:8). It seems to have been a common practice among the chosen people to meditate

on the word in the quiet of the night (Ps 4:4; 63:6). Twice we read in Luke's Gospel that the Mother of the Lord, the perfect woman, pondered the word in her heart (Lk 2:19, 51).

9. *Loving contemplative immersion*. As we shall explain farther on, our Christocentric contemplation is a divinely given growth in mental prayer, given when we are ready, not before. It is a superior way of communing with God, a way that goes beyond images, concepts, and words. When it grows normally, it becomes deep, beautiful, intimate, love-filled. It is completely given by God, and so we call it infused contemplation. More details later. For now we will explain how the biblical message charmingly speaks of this kind of communing with the Lord.

We should observe that this inspired account does not mention ideas and words, for this new communing cannot be expressed verbally. Scripture calls it the "one thing", the most important human activity, namely, gazing on the beauty and loveliness of the Lord (Ps 27:4). It is living through love in the divine presence (Ps 21:6; Eph 1:4). At dawn we hold ourselves open to receive from the Lord (Ps 5:3; 92:2). We taste how good he is, the biblical way of saying that we experience for ourselves the very goodness of God (Ps 34:8–10), and we drink from the divine river of delight. We do not have to reason and think ideas: we receive his joy in a wordless way. This can also be expressed by our being quiet and experiencing that he is the Lord of all (Ps 46:10). Sts. Paul and Peter explain that we then pray so deeply that words cannot describe the experience (Rom 8:26; 1 Pet 1:8).

Not surprisingly, in this prayer we are transformed from one glory to another (2 Cor 3:18). We rest in God, our sole ultimate fulfillment, a fulfillment that begins here in this life (Ps 62:1–2, 5–7). The psalmist speaks of pining with love for God and finding in him his sole delight, the surpassing joy of being close to his God (Ps 73:25–26, 28). As we grow toward this loving immersion we are more and more sharing in and reliving Jesus' habitual and long periods of solitude, being absorbed in the Father through their common love, the Holy Spirit (Mk 1:35; Lk 6:12; 5:16, and so on).

10. *Delighting and rejoicing.* The community of both Testaments, Old and New alike, is remarkable in how frequently it expresses the intense joy the faithful are routinely expected to experience in the course of their daily lives. They seem to know nothing of boredom. This delight is mentioned over and over again in the psalter and in the prayer life of the Church. Our hearts and our flesh are to thrill with gladness in the living God as we sing alleluias to him as the very source of the thrilling (Ps 84:2). We exult in this Lord and in his marvels (Ps 9:1–16; 40:5; 75:1), and this we do with endless shouts of exultation and triumph (Ps 5:11; 20:5). With the exception of the Lenten season the Church through the year repeats in her daily liturgies these shouts of alleluia.

11. *The sound of music.* As though all this were not enough, both the inspired word and the contemporary Church elicit the resources of musical talents and instruments. As one of our recent popes remarked, echoing St. Augus-

tine, they who sing pray twice. All this God's people did with gusto. They sang the wonders the Lord had wrought in salvation history (Ps 105:1-5). Their prayer was expressed with music sounding to their King (Ps 47:1, 5-6; 57:7-9; 59:16-17). At least on occasion they set aside timidity in their celebrations: they praised the transcendent greatness of God with lyre and harp, strings and reeds, the beating of drums and the clashing of cymbals —and yes, with dancing, too, in praise of his name. For example, David and the community "danced before Yahweh with all their might, singing to the accompaniment of lyres, harps, tambourines, castanets, and cymbals" (2 Sam 6:5; Ps 87:7; 149:3; 150:1-6). Nothing dreary and dull here. Perhaps they were praying three or four times!

All of this makes sense. Anyone profoundly in love is inclined (perhaps even driven) to sing to the beloved. As Vatican Council II put it, the Church in her liturgy is "vox sponsae ad Sponsum"—the voice of the bride (singing) to her Spouse. Which is another way in which the Church is telling us that we are to be head over heels in love, that is, men and women of profoundly deep prayer.

12. *Amen!* In Greek, Latin, and Hebrew, "amen" meant "yes indeed, certainly, so may it be". And so our last words here are reserved to Jesus and his Mother. Both insisted on the identification of their and our wills with that of the Father: "Our Father. . . . Your will be done. . . ." and "Let it be done to me according to your word." Yes, amen: let your will be done. So be it. Identifying our will with the divine will is the very heart of sanctity. And the more perfect the identification, the more lofty

the holiness. Both the transforming union in contemplative prayer and the practice of heroic virtue (there is an intercausality between these two traits of perfect sanctity) involve complete identification with the divine will.

The single word "amen" is an affirmation of what God positively wills or of his permitting something to occur (for a still greater good). It reminds us of St. Francis de Sales remarking that if we knew all that God knows, we would will to happen exactly what does happen (see also Rom 8:28). Amen, the conclusion of many prayers in the Church's liturgy, is a proclamation of the all-knowing wisdom of the Father, Son, and Holy Spirit. (For more on this variety of biblical prayer, see CCC 2623–49.)

Traits of biblical prayer

The best of our scientists and theologians emphatically affirm that beauty is a powerful pointer to truth (see the author's *The Evidential Power of Beauty*). Even a cursory reading of this present chapter makes clear that no other religion, oriental or occidental, begins to compare in its account of human relating to the divine with the elegance, splendor, and richness we find in Sacred Scripture. The magnificence of this inspired description of prayer is, of course, part and parcel of the whole splendor of the trinitarian plan of salvation. We can therefore summarize some of the overall traits of the scriptural account.

Our twelve types of prayer combine characteristics that no merely human minds have come close to conceiving, let alone implementing. On the one hand, there is tremen-

dous, even unspeakable joy, love, delight, a huge optimism, and, on the other hand, all of this is happily and
confidently related to our weakness, sinfulness, suffering,
pain, and failures. No other literature produced by our
human race has been so real, so encouraging, so healing,
so utterly satisfying to sincere and thoughtful men and
women.

Another combination that no Aristotle, no Plato, no
Socrates, no oriental master has been able to conceive
is the glorious interweaving of an awesomely vivid and
reverent appreciation of God's endless power, might, and
majesty together with a touching and tender familiarity
we may have with him. Infinitely mighty though he be,
this Lord is always caring and loving—even to the extent
of the appalling scene of the crucifixion.

If you or I had composed a book of prayer with no help
from revelation, we would have made it I/me-centered.
We would have been its focus and center of gravity. But
biblical prayer has it right: it is rightly and utterly God-
centered, while at the same time it shows the Lord tenderly caring for us as the apple of his eye. What could
present so beautiful a picture as that of the father running
to meet his returning prodigal son with a hug and a tender
kiss? Then, too, while the psalmist is filled with awe at
the wonders of creation, he is struck even more with the
beauty of the divine Artist. Consequently, he overflows
with ecstatic delight. We have here combined supreme
optimism and entire realism.

Finally, who of us would have thought of prayer becoming continual and yet at the same time leaving us free

to give unhindered attention to other people and to our work? Thus it becomes when the faithful reach the summit, the transforming union.

We are now prepared to proceed to the second part of our primer: the interpersonal union/intimacy itself. We will sketch how it normally begins, grows, and reaches fullness. Remember that to appreciate acorns, we need to understand something about oak trees.

PART TWO

INTERPERSONAL UNION/INTIMACY

6

Getting Started

Since the title of this book is *Prayer Primer*, it is likely that either you or someone else considered you to be a beginner. Perhaps this volume was a gift to you—or possibly you picked it up in a bookstore or at the back of your parish church. In any event, let us presume that you are a novice in the matter of communing with God.

Who are beginners?

Our first answer to this question is that we do not envision chronological age to be the primary factor. God can touch a child or teenager deeply. While I trust our reflections may be useful to the latter, I hope they may be equally helpful to young adults and to their elders. In this context of prayer a beginner is anyone who wants God but is probably uneasy or insecure about the whole matter. Often questions abound: What am I supposed to do when I pray? Is prayer mostly or only reciting formulas? Especially, what is meditation? And contemplation? Are they for me? What does it mean "to grow in prayer"?

How much should a person pray each day or week? How do you fill in the time? Can busy people really be prayerful?

A competent teacher in any field takes the students where they are, not where ideally they should be. This is one reason, among many, why Sacred Scripture presents the abundance of prayer themes we considered in our last chapter. These themes, and many others we did not mention, suggest the wide variety of step-off points from which men and women (and teenagers) may begin to seek the Lord more earnestly.

Starting points

How do people get interested enough in prayer to begin wondering about the idea as it may apply to them? What might prompt a person to pick up this prayer primer in the first place? Or read an advertisement promoting it? One human starting point (we are presupposing divine grace) can be a slowly developing feeling of emptiness at not having God at all, or not having him deeply. Worldly people tend to smother this anxiety in their deep center by an increasing multiplication of excitements and pleasures. But thoughtful men and women perceive that something is fundamentally wrong. They sense that we are not made to be vacuums. Their lives may have little or no experienced meaning, and they clearly are not happy. Touched by grace, they begin to turn to the sole quenching of the nameless thirst at the core of their person. That is, they begin to turn to God.

Akin to this starting point is the second, a life of pervasive and serious sins: arrogance, power seeking, lust, avarice, abuse of others. By itself, of course, sin does not result in prayer, but its damaging results understandably lead to emptiness, guilt, and disgust—each of which can become a fertile field in which God can work the beginnings of repentance in an honest and humble person.

The third launching point for prayer is a weariness with one's own mediocrity. In this spiritual and moral lukewarmness there is no complete rejection of God. The person does want him, but only feebly. This is the half-hearted individual who makes little effort to avoid venial sins, who willingly shows impatience, gossips about others' faults, indulges in overeating, gives in to petty vanities about appearance, accomplishments, or talents, makes little effort to overcome laziness or grouchiness (Rev 3:2–3, 14–21). Mediocre people may on occasion and through grace respond to a powerful homily, or a shining example of a family member or friend, or to an experience at Mass —anything that may arouse them from their moral listlessness. Prayer may sprout even in this unpromising garden. It could sprout from these pages. But that depends on free will and response. God forces no one.

The final step-off point we may mention is the gratuitous goodness of God. He can and on occasion does touch a person deeply and suddenly with an astonishing experience that is never forgotten. This gift was given to St. Augustine. It also happened to John Henry Newman when he was a teenager. These profound touches can trigger, with no apparent preparation, a burning love or light or insight or thirsting for the divine love and beauty. A prayer life is suddenly born. Two cautions: The recipient still needs to do a lot of hard work in living a serious spiritual life—growth is not automatic. The second caution: No one ought to wait for or count on an extraordinary experience in order to get moving. This would be rash, presumptuous, extremely foolish. One would be inviting disaster.

Deepening conversion

The fundamental condition for an authentic relationship with God is changing course from our original egocentrism to the real Center of reality, God himself. Beginning a serious prayer life is before all else to begin conversion. The reversal we have in mind here is a moral/spiritual turning from selfishness to a love for truth, goodness, beauty—this is to begin a turn to God.

In the long run shams never work. Any authentic relationship, and this includes coming closer to the God we want to love, involves shedding selfishness, making him, and not our own pleasures and whims, the center of our gravity.

If in our choices we equivalently say, "Lord, I do not want your plan for me; I want my own will and desires. I know better than you what is good for me", no advancing relationship is possible. If a man thinks of a woman, "I want you for the pleasures you give me; I am not concerned about your eternal good, your deep worth as a person; I will not sacrifice for you and your welfare", then of course any talk about real love is mere pretense. Lust is exploitation, not love. Cheap words of admiration and affection do not remove the sham. Everyone knows this. Or should know it.

Jesus was right on target when in the first recorded words of his public ministry he proclaimed to the crowd, ''Be converted and welcome the gospel'' (Mk 1:15). Note well: the conversion comes before the welcome. This conversion must be 180 degrees from the self-centered idols we have been discussing to the real God. When sinners give up their false gods and begin to love truth, goodness, and beauty, a radical reversal takes place. They begin to be attracted to the splendors of the gospel message.

The more deeply we are converted, the more we welcome Beauty himself and all he has to say. We are prepared for a deepening prayer life.

But you might remark, ''I am too weak to do this radical thing with my life, and I am not sure I want to do it. What then?'' The answer to that problem is that, of course, you (and all of us) are too weak for any conversion, let alone so radical a one. But this is one of the reasons Scripture provides us with so many examples of how to pray for the help we so direly need. Say those prayers sincerely, and you are on the way. See chapter 5, perhaps repeatedly.

But we need also to accompany the prayer with action. Begin where you are. If you are filled with pride and vanity, look upon Jesus spit upon, struck, whipped to blood, nailed to the cross for love of you. Pray about this astonishing example, and make some decisions about your life and your priorities. Get busy now.

If pride shows itself in your refusing to accept the Church's teaching, even though the Lord said to her, "He who hears you, hears me, and he who rejects you, rejects me", learn some humility: you do not know better than God what is true and good for you. Or if you live for fame or admiration, give it up—and pray that you may give it up.

If lust is the problem, reflect on the emptiness and disgust you experience within yourself immediately after you sin, whether you be alone or with another person. Reflect on how you fail to see and honor the deep beauty of another person and reduce her/him to a mere means to your ignoble purpose. Reflect on how you eternally endanger and damage another because of your lust. Pray that you have pure eyes, mind, heart. So also with other sins: ponder, pray, repent, receive the sacraments worthily.

So how does the sinner begin to pray? Wherever one is on the path to God, love for truth, goodness, and beauty, together with sincere efforts to put that love into action, provide the context for fruitful prayer. I suggest once again that you review chapter 5—you will find magnificent, inspired prayers you can make your own as you begin your serious pursuit of God.

Life-triggering prayer

We suppose now that you have begun a sincere prayer life. You may not be perfect yet, but you are on the way. So far, so good. But now you wonder, "How do I begin my daily prayers? Must I always read somebody else's words from a book or pamphlet? This question we shall discuss in our next chapter on vocal prayer. For now we shall be content with the more general problem: What sort of things can prompt prayer throughout the day?

First of all, we should realize that communing with God is not a mere formality, technique, or method. So, you may ask, how do we get started? The short answer is to be yourself. There is no one exclusive way. God is your supreme Beloved; be at home with him. He is here now. He loves you unimaginably more than you love yourself. "Cast your cares on him, and he will care for you" (1 Pet 5:7). You do your part, and he will do his.

Scripture tells us that we should pray through the day, but without neglecting our work or other people. All sorts of diverse happenings can remind us of the divine omnipresence and ignite a short sentiment directed to God. Suppose someone scowls at you. Simply say, "Lord, he is hurting; heal and comfort him." Someone else is gracious toward you. "Thank you, Jesus; I really did not deserve that." Or the day is hot and humid, or cold and stormy. "Gladly I join with you, Lord, in your freely embracing all aspects of our human situation." Or you are worried, or feel weary, or have a headache, or all three together at one time. "I welcome these tiny sufferings as small sharings in your being tortured to death through love for us." Dinner is tasty or the sunset is gorgeous. "Blessed are you, my God, for making this universe so delightful; it could have been dull and drab."

Yes, be yourself. Getting intimate with God is simple: nothing complex, contrived, artificial. All that is required

is good will, and you can have this merely by wanting it
. . . and then making some effort. And be sure to perse-
vere, to stick with it.

Once again: Who are beginners?

Before we bring this chapter to its close, we return to
the opening question we asked: Who are beginners in
prayer? Novices or veterans, we are all unworthy beggars,
unworthy even to appear before the unspeakable beauty
and goodness who is our God, let alone to converse with
him. Most people consider it a privilege simply to be
greeted by a famous person or to shake hands. Who of
us would not feel blessed to have a chat for ten minutes
with Augustine or Bernard or Thomas or Catherine or
Teresa or Thérèse? Yet it is the infinite Trinity, Lord of
all the saints with whom we chat at prayer. *The Imitation
of Christ* puts it well: "O Lord my God, You are all my
good, and who am I that I should dare speak to You?"
(book 3, chapter 3). We dare because by his tenderness in
Scripture he invites us over and over to have a chat with
him. Best of all, the Son of the Father admonishes us to
pray "Our Father . . ." and even to "pray always" (Mt
6:9–18; Lk 18:1). The chat may even be wordless, just
being with Someone who loves you unspeakably. (For
more on Jesus' teaching about prayer, see CCC 2607–
15; 2663–82.)

7

Vocal Prayer

We now take up the best known of all types of communing with God. Indeed, among many people it is the only kind of prayer they know—which poses a number of problems we shall address a bit farther on.

But first we must make the point that, even though we shall later speak of loftier contemplation, vocal prayer is good, needed, and important. Jesus himself taught that we should address God with human thoughts and words. "Ask and you shall receive", he said, and he taught us himself to say the Our Father. His Church offers us precious treasures in her Eucharistic Sacrifice and in the Liturgy of the Hours. She encourages lay people to join religious and clergy in enriching their lives at this daily banquet of her official prayer. Likewise the Church promotes private devotions such as the rosary, the way of the cross, and litanies.

Why do the Lord and his Church require vocal prayers even in saintly men and women who engage in meditation and/or deep contemplation? Obviously God does not need our expressed words, as though he could not hear the silent thoughts and desires of our minds and hearts. Nor does he need to be informed of our problems and petitions. It is we who need to express our inner life in worded forms. Why is this so? (In addition to these thoughts, see also CCC 2700–2704.)

A moment's observation provides the first explanation. People in trouble spontaneously voice their pain or problem in words, usually vocalized. It is the natural thing to do.

The second reason is likewise rooted in our human nature: We are bodily beings, not angels, and so we should express our prayers at times in bodily ways, that is, with readable and audible expressions. Further, we are social beings, and therefore we do these things together. Community requires that on occasion we share praise and worship with one another, and this calls for words and, sometimes, for ceremonies and gestures.

Thirdly, we need to support one another tangibly in our journey toward God, and the world needs our communal witness to the primacy of our Creator, whom we love and adore. Children in a family first learn about prayer in experiencing it with mother, father, and siblings.

Further, the best of our worded prayers instruct us and nourish our spiritual lives with the truth, goodness, and beauty they express. They teach the beginner how to commune with God and to take the first steps toward intimacy with him and with his Mother and the other saints. All these benefits are especially present in the Church's official worship. This we shall consider in chapter 10, dealing with the Liturgy of the Hours.

Types of vocal prayer

In addition to the official liturgy of the Church, there are a number of other kinds of worded prayer. The place of primacy among these must be assigned to eucharistic devotions that surround and extend the immense and powerful influence of the daily celebration of Mass. And so we have Benediction of the Blessed Sacrament, which through the centuries has been much prized and loved by the best of the faithful. Begun in the thirteenth century, Benediction is called a paraliturgical devotion (that is, like a liturgical celebration). Because the universal Church continues to be much in favor of fostering and promoting this devotion, the Holy See has recently simplified and deepened its beautiful ceremonies so that we may be enriched all the more.

We also have the annual solemn exposition of the Blessed Sacrament in parishes and religious houses "so that the local community may meditate on and adore more intensely the eucharistic mystery" (canon 942). This practice is a continuing development of the Forty Hours devotion established in 1592 by Pope Clement VIII. On national and international levels this same desire to intensify and further devotion to the Eucharist is seen in the many eucharistic congresses that are sponsored throughout the world on a periodic basis.

Likewise in the last two or three decades we have seen in our land a remarkable blossoming on the parish level of adoration of the Blessed Sacrament in an organized way. I can think of no explanation for this widespread phenomenon other than the grace of the Holy Spirit touching the laity and their pastors. In some parishes the adoration is sponsored at certain times each week. In other churches adoration is perpetual, twenty-four hours each day and night, seven days a week. These favored opportunities for eucharistic communion are not meant exclusively for vocal prayers, but also for quiet meditation and contemplative union with the risen Lord present in both his human and divine natures.

The way of the cross is another favorite devotion among many of the faithful, especially during Lent and on Fridays. Parishes usually have communal services for the way of the cross on the Fridays of Lent, and throughout the year we notice men and women individually pondering the Lord's passion as they go quietly from station to station. Over the centuries a large number of ways of making the stations have been proposed, and these ways are explained in booklets and pamphlets readily available in pamphlet racks at the back of churches and in Catholic bookstores.

The Jesus prayer is a traditional devotion based on the words of the blind beggar of Jericho: "Jesus, Son of David, have mercy on me" (Mk 10:47–48). The exact wording of the prayer varies—for example, another version is "Jesus, Son of the living God, be merciful to me, a sinner." Because of its solid content and the power of the Lord's name, it is a fine prayer. Likewise, it furthers love for our Savior, and it arouses genuine contrition. When an infused wordless communion with him begins, we then cease using the words and are content just to rest in him in a way that surpasses words.

Another unstructured type of worded prayer are the

brief, spontaneous sentiments that people coming closer to God are likely to sprinkle throughout the day, and even as they fall off to sleep at night. Anyone deeply in love with another readily and often thinks of the beloved. Since the indwelling Trinity is always present in the deepest center of our person (supposing we are in the state of grace) and always extending their listening ear to whatever is on our mind, it is perfectly natural and normal to share our spontaneous feelings, thoughts, and desires with Father, Son, and Holy Spirit: "I love you . . . Thank you for this little favor . . . Help me to show warmth to this unappealing person I see coming down the corridor . . . Blessed be your name! . . . I'm sorry I showed this impatience . . . Lord Jesus, I need you . . . I adore you in the nearest tabernacle . . . Do keep me gentle (or patient, or pleasant, or pure, or poor in spirit) . . . Help me to be temperate at this coming meal . . . I seek you with all my heart . . . I long and thirst for you . . . Give me a happy death . . . Help all missionaries . . . Bless my parents, friends, benefactors, enemies." These short ejaculations and others like them pierce the heavens—especially when they are sincere and fervent.

Multiplying vocal prayers: Problems and solutions

For all the reasons we have touched upon in this chapter, worded prayers are indeed important, and yet we must now look into a widespread difficulty, a difficulty common among sincere people, both lay and religious. I refer to the excessive multiplication of vocal prayers to the neglect of "pondering the word day and night" (Ps 1:2) and a contemplative immersion in the beauty of the Lord, the "one thing" we often speak about in this primer. We can overdo good things. Water is basic to human life, but too much of it in one place (the lungs) kills. Human speech is a marvelous gift from God. But if we use it to excess, for example, in idle words, the Lord tells us we shall give an account on judgment day (Mt 12:36).

What exactly, you may ask, is the problem here? If vocal prayers are precious, what then is wrong with saying many of them? The mistake here may be that one good activity when overdone squeezes out other duties that are also needed and perhaps more important. Work is good. Indeed it is an important duty. "Woe to me", said St. Paul, "if I do not proclaim the gospel" (1 Cor 9:16). But habitually working too much prevents other important activities: prayer, spiritual reading, needed rest, personal enrichment through experiencing truth, goodness, beauty. What I am saying here was said centuries ago by Jesus himself. When the apostles had been on the road proclaiming the word, and were being pressured by the peoples' needs so that they were not even able to eat, he told the apostles that they *must* go off and rest for a while (Mk 6:30–32). On another occasion he repeated what the psalmist had declared long before, namely that "gazing on the beauty of the Lord" is the most important thing anyone has to do in life (Lk 10:38–42). Lesser activities, good as they may be in themselves, may not habitually impede greater ones. Jesus himself did not permit his teaching and healing to hinder his habit of spending long periods of time in solitude communing with the Father.

He was even more explicit and blunt in directing us

that when we pray we should not babble like the pagans do, thinking that in using many words they will make themselves heard (see Mt 6:7, JB). Shortly after Vatican Council II Pope Paul VI, faithful to the Master's mind, admonished religious to cut down on the number of their vocal prayers and increase their time for mental prayer. Individually or communally some religious had long lists of vocal prayers they would recite every day, while they gave little time to contemplation, even though Scripture could not be more clear in stating that the latter is the top priority in a well-ordered life. It does not appear that many have heard or heeded the papal instruction, for not much has changed in many congregations.

This same problem is perhaps even more pronounced among sincere lay people who have not been instructed about meditation and its importance. They assume that to grow in prayer means to multiply words and devotions. Not realizing that the Lord, his Church, and the saints say just the contrary, they add diverse pious exercises one upon the other—and this on a daily basis. They mean well but do not grasp what they are missing, usually, we may presume, through lack of instruction in the classroom and from the pulpit.

Hints for improving vocal prayers

1. The quality of our prayers is more important than the quantity, the number of them. It is better to offer a few prayers with depth of attention and fervor than many repeated with little care or in a rushing way. Sts. Teresa of Avila and Francis de Sales have remarked that it is better

to say one Our Father or Hail Mary with inner attention and love than to recite many with a scattered mind and a tepid heart.

2. If, during vocal prayers to which you are not obliged, your mind and heart are drawn to meditation or contemplation, you are welcome to cease the worded prayers you had intended to offer. This is the advice of St. Francis de Sales, and he adds that God is more pleased with mental communion with him and that it is also more profitable for your soul (*Introduction to the Devout Life*, pt. 1, 1, 8). The saint rightly makes an exception for prayers of obligation, such as the Liturgy of the Hours for a priest.

3. It is wise before beginning personal prayers, and the Liturgy of the Hours as well, to pause a few moments to recollect yourself, that is, to gather your inner attention to what you are going to do.

4. In choosing among many possible private devotions, it is good to consider giving priority to the Liturgy of the Hours, if you can find the needed preliminary instruction. It is the official prayer of the universal Church, and since it is made up mostly of biblical thoughts and sentiments, it is immensely rich, beautiful, and moving. Likewise, it is wonderful to be in union with our brothers and sisters throughout the world and, together with them, to praise, love, and adore the Blessed Trinity. (For more see chapter 10.)

5. Our final suggestion returns us to the question people have who seek to follow the admonitions of Jesus, his Church, and her saints, that we not multiply vocal prayers beyond measure or babble with many words. Suppose these men and women value their favorite devotions and

are reluctant to give them up? Should they simply say goodbye to them?

No, not necessarily. An alternative plan would be to spread their many prayers over a longer period of time, a week or a month. Instead of forcing fifteen decades of the rosary and several litanies into one day, plus intercessions for the missions, the conversion of sinners, reparation for sin, and on and on, they could distribute these among a longer period of time. In this way they retain their preferences and yet provide more amply for meditative and contemplative communing with the Lord.

Are your prayers answered?

Jesus assures us emphatically that if we seek, we shall find (not just perhaps); if we ask, it will be given to us; if we knock, it will be opened (Mt 7:7–8). Yet, you may wonder, what are we to think of the petitions we make that do not seem to be answered?

Several observations are in order. First of all, the Lord is supposing the normal situation, namely, that we are praying as we ought to pray. There are conditions to be fulfilled—as is normal in other human relationships as well. The first one is that we seek before all else our greatest good and the genuine welfare of others. If that is lacking, what else matters? Scripture teaches us plainly that if we seek the Lord with all our heart and all our soul, we shall find him (Deut 4:29). Saints always find God, and in finding him they obtain everything else they need. The psalmist tells us to be sure that the Lord does wonders for his faithful ones (Ps 4:3, JB). So we need to ask: Am I faithful? The New Testament insists that whatever we ask for we will receive *because* we keep his commandments and live the kind of life God knows is best for us (1 Jn 3:22). Are you and I living that kind of life?

The second and third conditions for our prayers to be answered are included in the first one. Namely, we are to ask with full trust in the Lord (Jas 1:5–8), and we are to seek the right things, what is best for ourselves and for others (Jas 4:2–3). We are to put first things first and ask for genuine goods.

One further question: Suppose we ask for the conversion of a sinner, surely a good and holy petition, and yet he does not give up the wrongdoing or does not return to the Church? What has happened? Has God answered this prayer? Yes, indeed. He has given the transgressor all the graces he needs for a complete conversion; the Lord has responded to the prayer. Yet he leaves the sinner free to use the graces given or not to use them. God forces himself on no one. St. Monica, the mother of the tremendous Augustine, prayed for twenty years for the conversion of her son. The Holy Spirit was working in his mind and heart for two decades (thus responding to the mother's tears and petitions), and when her son finally said a complete Yes, he was mightily converted, not only to the state of grace, but eventually to the very heights of heroic holiness and the transforming union of prayer. Worthy prayers are indeed answered.

8

Meditation

Perhaps we should begin this chapter by responding to a difficulty some people may have regarding its inclusion in a book professedly written for beginners. This problem could readily occur among those who view mental prayer as reserved for the few, the elite. Considerable numbers of laymen and women assume without question that prayer means vocal prayer only, and they have the company of a few clergy. From available evidence it seems rare that one hears a homily on the subject of this chapter or on our next one, contemplation.

It is not surprising, of course, that if the faithful seldom receive instruction on mental prayer, they assume either that it does not exist or at least that it is not meant for them. What is odd is that presumably well-educated and religiously minded leaders would not be aware that the first two verses of the inspired book of prayer, the psalter, plainly declare blessed the faithful who ponder the word of the Lord day and night (Ps 1:1–2). That is high praise indeed. All of us in every state in life, young and old alike, are to taste and drink deeply and thus to experience how good God is (Ps 34:5, 8). This is the language of advancing contemplative prayer. A moment's reflection reminds us that the Church herself places these words, and many others like them, on everyone's lips over and over in the liturgy. It is no exaggeration to express astonishment that pastors and spiritual leaders only too often seem to be unaware of the dynamite in these texts and/or of what they mean—or that they are at all important. Clearly they express the Church's mind, and that of the saints in all states of life, in saying that meditation and contemplation are for everyone. (See CCC 2705–8; FW, pp. 199–216.)

To put the matter in mild and gentle terms, a prayer primer should at least let beginners know where they are headed, where the goal is, and then offer a few glimpses of meditation's beauty and efficacy in bringing them into a divine intimacy, which normally is consummated in the sublime realms of advanced contemplative communion with the indwelling Trinity. We will need also to take at least a peek at how this growing prayer increases immensely the good we can do for others. After all, when we know the fullness of a living being or activity, we understand better the beginnings of it. Oak trees tell us what acorns are about, and knowing mature adults helps us appreciate babies all the more.

One further point. Experience has shown that informed, dedicated teachers, parents, and catechists can easily teach meditation to four- and five-year-old youngsters. Using kiddie terms and reminding themselves that the child's attention span is brief, they could, for example, set an atmosphere by asking the children to close their eyes and then say to them something like the following. "Now I am going to talk to you a little bit about God, who is living in each one of you. Then we are going to think about him, love him, and silently speak to him." The instructor then explains a new theme each day for this inner conversation. Slowly she lengthens the time from perhaps thirty seconds to two or three minutes after several weeks. When the children are ready, they may take turns in leading the group. It can be amazing what they will come up with. Interspersed, short, silent times give the youngsters the opportunity to share personally with their Lord.

Not surprisingly, normal children take to what is going on as fish welcome water. Their minds are fresh and uncomplicated, and their imaginations vivid. They are inclined to wonder and to love in their own fashion. If they can so readily learn meditation and grow in intimacy with God, anyone can.

What then is meditation?

Just as you and I get to know people by meeting, listening, and speaking to them, so in meditation we get to know God interpersonally by conversing with him in a quiet place: "When you pray, go into your private room, close the door and pray to your Father in that secret place" (Mt 6:6) We listen to him speaking to us through the beauties of nature, Sacred Scripture, the texts of the liturgy, the lives and writings of the saints. Pointedly Jesus declared in completely explicit terms that we hear him when we listen to the Church teaching in his name: "He who hears you, hears me" (Lk 10:16). In meditation we ponder what he says to us in all these ways, and then we respond with our inner thoughts, applications, and words. It is a mental conversation between two friends coming closer and, as time goes on, becoming more and more intimate.

This silent conversation is only the beginning stage of becoming more and more familiar with our unspeakable Creator dwelling in our soul. Meditation is prayer in the human manner. By that we mean that it is we who read or reflect on suitable thoughts that will arouse our adoration, praise, requests, thanksgiving, expressions of sorrow and love. (See also FW, pp. 49–50.) When the person is ready, the Lord gives a new kind of awareness of himself that we can only receive, not produce of ourselves. We will explain this in our next chapter. For now we consider only meditation.

Jesus, focal point of meditation

Even though you probably suspect that the primary subject for our meditation is the person of the Incarnate Word of the Father, we need to emphasize that both Scripture and the example of the saints proclaim loudly and clearly that we are to center our attention on him and the mysteries of his life. He himself declared that they who see him see the Father (Jn 14:9); that is, he is himself the perfect picture of what God is like. He has likewise laid it down that no one goes to the Father except through the Son (Jn 14:6).

St. Teresa of Avila advised her nuns that turning their inner eyes upon Jesus in all of the details of his life was the best way to begin their meditative prayer. Among those actions of his, she loved most of all to reflect on some aspect of his passion and death, for there we find the most splendid picture of totally selfless love. St. Francis de Sales taught beginners that often meditating on him fills their souls with his person, so that they more and more begin to think, speak, and act just as he did.

Since Jesus himself habitually spent long hours in prayerful solitude with the Father (Lk 5:16), and yet with no excessive "babbling of many words", he was telling us by word and example that much meditative/contemplative prayer is indeed the "one thing" in our lives. Any consistent theist must agree with him.

What else might you ponder within the temple of your being where the Blessed Trinity dwells? Big things and little things: Why are you on this planet? What does it profit you to get everything you want in this life, if you end up in an eternal disaster? (Mt 16:26) What does becoming perfect mean? (Mt 5:48) How do you become a saint? What else matters?

What are some of the little things you might chat about with Father, Son, and Holy Spirit? Being more pleasant at supper this evening . . . Visiting somebody who is sick . . . Overcoming your temper . . . Eating fewer sweets . . . Getting over vanity.

Because indwelling Beauty should be everyone's supreme Beloved, however, we especially profess our love and adoration, simply and sincerely.

What about methods for meditation?

Most beginners need an explanation that answers their question, "How do I go about making a meditation?"

Many approaches have been proposed over the centuries. Among them are those of St. Ignatius of Loyola, Father Olier, St. John Baptist de la Salle, St. Teresa of Avila. A well-stocked Catholic bookstore should have a number of contemporary pamphlets or books explaining sundry ways of going about meditation.

These methods vary from complex to simple: from many steps in the procedures to very few. I prefer to teach beginners a non-complex approach, and in this we will follow the mind of St. Teresa. In any stage of prayer loving is more important than reasoning. As she put it, "The important thing is not to think much, but to love much." (See FW, pp. 82–83.)

So what would a simple procedure be like? The first step is to choose a quiet place and a suitable time: "Be quiet and know that I am God" (Ps 46:10). Jesus taught this first detail by example and by word. He himself habitually went off to be alone "long before dawn" or even through the night where he could give full attention to his Father (Mk 1:35; Lk 5:16; 6:12). And he told lay people that in their prayer they should make a quiet place in their home, "close the door", and pray to the Father in this domestic solitude (Mt 6:6). Monks and nuns do this on a grand scale in their monasteries, and many people do it in an intensive way during silent retreats.

It is extraordinary that the Creator of billions of huge galaxies, each of which on average contains more billions of enormous suns, should descend to the tiny detail of telling us to "close the door" of our prayer place. This is an awesome tribute to our individual importance and that of communing with the Father: we and our prayer are more splendid than all the galaxies taken together!

The second step is inwardly to gather ourselves together in mind and heart just as athletes speak of mental concentration needed to perform well. This gentle recollection of oneself can be done by recalling the divine presence . . . or the Holy Name of Jesus . . . or the indwelling mystery . . . or the Eucharist, if one is in church or chapel . . . or an episode from the passion or any one of dozens of other scenes from the Lord's life.

Thirdly, one provides input, usually by reading a passage from Scripture, or (for example) from *The Imitation of Christ*, or a paragraph from the life of a saint, or a small portion of the day's liturgy.

Then come our responses to what has been read: applying it to our life and conversing with the Lord about it. The reading, pondering, and applying prepare us for the heart of Christian meditation: adoring, loving, praising, thanking, and sorrowing with inner, quiet words. These affections of will and heart are the chief aim of meditation, which is not a mere pious study about religious matters.

Finally, the resolution. We determine to do something specific (beginning today) about what we have been pondering. We resolve to change and grow so that our actions may match our prayer.

Quick tips for using a method

1. Method in meditation is like a scaffolding used to construct a building. It is a means to the end, not the end itself.

2. Just as in the case of scaffolding, prayer methods are not meant to be permanent. When they have achieved their purpose, we leave them aside. Otherwise they can impede more simple and better prayer. This we will explain in our next chapter. (See also SSD, p. 187.) We may add here several other tips from SSD, p. 182:

[3.] Meditative prayer should be calm and unhurried. There is no set amount of material to be covered. One sentence or paragraph may at times serve for an hour or a week of reflection and inner dialogue with God.

[4.] Beginners may overemphasize thinking at prayer. Imagination and reasoning have their places, especially in the early stages, but at any stage of development love is the core of communion.

[5.] Dialoguing with the indwelling Trinity includes other types of affectivity which are naturally sparked by diverse reflections: praising, sorrowing, yearning, thanking, petitioning.

[6.] Simplicity is in order. One should not be bewildered by an excessive concern with techniques, steps and procedures.

[7.] One should pay comparatively little attention to the method itself. Such a preoccupation can obstruct the Holy Spirit during the actual time of prayer.

[8.] Prolonged difficulty with a given procedure might suggest another approach, or a combination of other approaches. Consultation with one's guide at this point would be wise.

[9.] When one finds oneself united to God in a simple

loving attention or yearning, the methods should be left aside. One has what they are meant to bring about.

10. Scripture says not a word about techniques for prayer, not a word about oriental or centering ways to empty the mind. Rather our Christian meditation aims at filling our minds and hearts with pondering God's word in the books of creation and revelation. It is meant gradually to lead the beginner to something better, namely, to drinking the goodness and beauty of God in a wordless way. We are to grow to a radiant absorption in him farther down the road. Meditation prepares the novice for contemplative communing with the indwelling Trinity.

There are a few people who never seem quite able to pray meditatively. St. Teresa was one of them. Their difficulty may be the lack of a vivid imagination, or, more likely, they may have already progressed to a simple manner with God and go to him with unaffected love. Perhaps the best advice for most of these people is to pray as they can pray, not to try what they cannot do. Hence, for these few simply to abide in the divine presence without being concerned about producing images and reasonings leaves them open to whatever the Lord chooses to give. Competent spiritual direction here is a great help.

Specific steps

To meditate successfully we first of all choose a suitable time and then find or provide for ourselves a place of solitude, and this with determination, not a mere wish. Thinking of an ordinary home setting, Jesus himself recommends (as we have already noted) that we go to our

private room, close the door, and pray to the Father in secret. This can be difficult for parents with small children,
but it can be done. Saintly couples, past and present, do
it. They are determined. The Holy Father with six billion
people to be concerned about is far more time pressured
than any of us. Yet Pope John Paul II is careful to provide
frequent times for prayer. Even more: the Master of us
all, who during his public life was infinitely more needed
by others than we are, himself did what he told us to do:
"He would habitually go off where he could be alone
and pray" (Lk 5:16).

Lodged, then, in suitable solitude, our second step is
to begin to commune with God just as we begin talking
to anyone: we notice the presence of the person we are
addressing. Because this Lord is infinite light, paradoxically we cannot see him either with ordinary vision or
with our mind, so we need to make a special effort to
recall his natural omnipresence. But we also remind ourselves of his new supernatural presence in our very beings
by grace: our indwelling Guests. If we are in church or
chapel, we adore our risen Lord in the Eucharist. During
my high school days in Minneapolis the brothers would
begin each class by declaring: "Remember that we are in
the holy presence of God." Then we would say the vocal
prayer that began our class period. This practice struck
me then, and I have never forgotten it. It was simple, but
powerful, a fine way to begin any prayer.

Step number three is to say slowly some brief vocal
prayer: the Our Father or the Hail Mary or the Glory Be
or some other favorite one. Another alternative is to use
one's own words: "Lord, come to me; I need you . . .

Jesus, I want to love you with all my heart: help me to know how to speak with you in the center of my being . . . From my heart I wish to adore you, praise and love you . . ."

Input is step number four. You are now prepared to read something that may help your pondering and inner mental conversation with your indwelling Lord. You may read a small section from the Gospel accounts of Jesus' passion, his being whipped at the pillar, for example. Or it could be the Lord instructing the crowd on the mountainside, or instituting the Eucharist at the last supper, or conversing with the apostles, or in his risen glory coming through closed doors. Input could be your imagining yourself on your deathbed during your last hour in this life: How will things look to you then, or how would you pray at that moment? Or you could read a passage from *The Imitation of Christ*, the life of a saint, a verse or two from St. Paul or from a psalm.

Step number five: you ponder the passage, apply it to yourself, draw conclusions that fit your life, aims, and person. Most of all you talk over all this with the Master in your mind and will. Use your own thoughts, desires, petitions, inner words. Be simple. Be yourself. Be sure not to omit what we call the affections of the will: adoring, praising, repenting, thanking, asking. These affective responses are the very heart of Christian meditation. But be inwardly still, too, when that is your inclination: "Be quiet and know that I am God" (Ps 46:10). You are growing in intimacy with your Creator.

Finally, you make a concrete resolution: What am I going to do about all of this in the concrete details of my daily life? Things must change for the better if we are to grow in prayer. A vague wish to improve is not enough. Because meditation is at the core of coming closer to God (and therefore to others as well), it should lead to tangible results in the practical order of our behavior. Hence, ordinarily you want to conclude this daily prayer period with some specific resolution to improve, to grow in some virtue or get rid of some fault. "I will be ready for this annoying situation with my husband (wife) when it may occur today; I will be gentle even if firm." Or the resolution could be "when she (he) nags at me today, I shall be patient, or if I judge it proper to respond in some way, I will make it a point to be loving in my manner." Fidelity to meditation should affect life-style, and it therefore introduces a deeper happiness into a marriage, a convent, or a rectory.

Before leaving prayer time it is good to thank the Lord for the privilege of communing with him. And a few requests for help in carrying out the particular resolution are also advisable.

Subjects for meditation

In step number four above we said a few words about input for reflection. A bit more needs to be added. God is the author of two books that bountifully provide numberless topics for pondering: the book of created reality, our awesome universe, and the inspired book of the Scriptures. First, creation. If one delves deeply enough into it, every reality in our cosmos is seen to be splendid beyond our wildest expectations: a grain of sand, an atom, a living cell, a leaf, a bird, a star, a galaxy. It is no exaggeration to say that each of these things is astonishing. Always we find that the more we discover, the more we find endless vistas of what we did not expect and more of what we still do not know. Scientists constantly experience this phenomenon. If we are vibrantly alive to reality, we learn that there is no end to what can and should trigger awe, wonder, praise, thanksgiving, and love. (See also EPB, pp. 129–237.)

The second divinely authored meditation book is Sacred Scripture. Splendid as are the marvels of our universe all the way from the incredibly tiny to the vastly enormous, and all that lies in between, far more awesome and enriching are the truths of divine revelation. The Author of these two books has made nothing boring or prosaic. Boredom comes not from reality but from people who are only half alive. The truths of this second source can be read from Scripture itself, from any solid theology book or biblical commentary, from the lives of the saints, and from the best spiritual reading, mainly from the classics. For example, you have noticed in this primer references to "CCC", the *Catechism of the Catholic Church*, for further developments of what we are explaining in these pages. This single volume has literally thousands of meditation subjects full of grace, truth, and beauty. Rich mines are available for the asking. It is up to you to take advantage of them. (See also FW, pp. 50–51, and EPB, pp. 241–349.)

When and for how long should you pray?

Most beginners in meditative prayer seem to find the morning the best time for communing with God. Yet Scripture speaks of people conversing with God at many diverse times: in the early morning, late at night, before a task, in special need or danger, indeed, continually. There are two rules of thumb that help in answering the question of what is the best time for meditation: one is to pray when you pray best; the other is to pray when you can, that is, when it is possible or feasible.

The first guide: Pray when you pray best. Some people are early birds, while others are night owls. However, experience seems to show that most men and women meditate best in the morning before they begin their work day. They are more rested and fresh. They are less distracted by the needs and happenings of the day. The world (and probably their home as well) is more quiet.

The second guide: Pray when it is possible or feasible. A mother obviously cannot retreat into solitude when the baby is awake, crying, and/or hungry; nor a father when he is consulting with a client at the office.

These rules of thumb should be combined with a bit of ordinary psychology: it is best to establish a solid habit, a usual time. While there can be exceptions for good reasons, too easily shifting times for meditation can lead to procrastination and eventual neglect.

How long in duration should your mental prayer period be each day? This question cannot be answered wisely by advising a certain set limit for all beginners. Ideally a spiritual director who knows the directee's life situation and capacities would be a helpful guide here. One principle to follow is that one begins with the amount of time that usually can be implemented, perhaps ten, fifteen, or twenty minutes. It is better to under-commit than to over-commit. Fidelity to what we decide is important. Breaking a resolution without a good reason is both psychologically and spiritually damaging to growth and perseverance.

When the person is ready, the amount of time can be increased by perhaps ten-minute increments; most people would not find this too difficult. The goal is to develop a steady, habitual discipline that begins slowly but grows solidly, so that daily meditation becomes as natural to you and as much a part of your day as breathing is. This discipline is a means; a deeper relationship with your indwelling Lord is the end. We want to avoid a feast/famine pattern of prayer. It will not hold up under the influence of our constantly fluctuating feelings.

St. Francis de Sales recommended that lay people devote one hour to their daily meditation and if possible that it be in the early morning, a time when they are rested, refreshed, and less distracted. If a beginner finds that an hour is more than can be handled, he may, I think, start with less, but with the expectation that he will extend this favored time with his Creator, who loves him without measure.

Benefits of Christocentric meditation

As I have noted in chapter 5, the psalter, the inspired book of prayer, begins with two verses that proclaim that the

person who meditates on the word of the Lord day and
night is in a blessed condition (Ps 1:1–2). Why is this so?
First of all, a review of what we have said in this chapter makes clear that a prayerful pondering on the two
books of divine instruction deepens interpersonal intimacy with Father, Son, and Holy Spirit. This is why human beings who love each other seek to share with each
other the most important issues and realities in their lives.
In these sharings they become more selfless, loving, generous. Needless to say, they also enjoy each other more
richly. So also by meditation beginners grow in knowing
and loving their God. They become more dear to him,
and he to them.

Secondly, as our prayer deepens, so does supernatural
insight. We penetrate into the mysteries of our destiny
and the whole purpose of our life. Love bestows light
(1 Jn 4:7–8). We see our human relationships and the
rest of reality much more realistically. We see things in
proportion and perspective: seeing big things as big and
petty things as petty.

Thirdly, anyone who grows in love grows in happiness,
even to the point of "rejoicing in the Lord always" (Phil
4:4). The saints are like this.

Our fourth benefit is that the closer we are to the Trinity, the better we deal with suffering, even acute suffering. "For those who love God all things work together
for the good", said St. Paul (Rom 8:28). We all suffer
one thing or another, sometimes several difficulties at the
same time. Some people become cynical and bitter, even
ugly, in their pains and problems. If we join Jesus in his
being horrendously tortured to death for us, we grow

rapidly in love and therefore in joy as we bear our crosses with him.

Fifthly, meditation brings richness to both our liturgical celebrations and our private vocal prayers. It thus diminishes our tendencies to be mindless and routine, just "rattling off many words".

Sixthly, meditation strengthens us to do well whatever we do because it sharpens our motivation to be what we ought to be and to act as we ought to act—with enthusiasm, love, generosity, and zeal.

And this brings us to our final benefit: We do others far more good when we ourselves are close to God. The best thing husbands and wives, fathers and mothers, can do for each other and for their children is to become saints, men and women of burning prayer. Their effectiveness multiplies and snowballs. The impact of their words and actions is not only stronger—it is eternal. Indeed happy are those who ponder the word day and night.

9

Contemplation

If you have a problem with the title of this chapter being in a book intended for beginners in prayer, most likely you have company. Since contemplation is an advanced development of communing with God, why do we devote a section to it in a primer? Actually we are not going to say a great deal about this advancing prayer, but only what beginners should know in order to grow from where they are to where they want some day to be. Hence, we begin by offering a few answers to our question.

Why this chapter?

Our first response is that in any worthwhile journey most of us want to know where our destination is and how we are to get to it. We also like to know whether the trip is worth all the trouble and expense.

The second reason is that in living things (and prayer is our supremely living activity), we understand the beginnings fully only when we grasp their mature, complete stage of growth. We see the meaningfulness of a tadpole adequately only when we have seen an adult frog and all it can do. We appreciate the first steps of the spiritual life to the extent that we understand and come closer to living the virtues heroically well. We appreciate where meditation is leading us only if we grasp something of contemplative communing with the indwelling Trinity. Moreover, both our private and liturgical prayers take on a whole new dimension when we understand something of their inner life and vitality, and the more deeply we appreciate this, the more fruitful they are likely to be.

Thirdly, we have already noted that when sincere people know little or nothing of meditative and contemplative prayer, they often assume that there is no other prayer but vocal. Then many of them burden themselves with whole lists of words and formulas, leaving no time for deepening their interpersonal relationship with the Lord. If this volume had nothing about meditation and contemplation, we would be reinforcing this sad error. It would be like making a map that explains only the beginning of a trip.

Fourthly, knowing the beauty of a deep immersion in God and how it opens the path to heroic holiness, and that it is meant for everyone, we are encouraged to make the sacrifices entailed in making it possible.

Lastly, contemplative prayer can be taught effectively even to young people who are living the gospel with generosity. Thus they should know enough about it to recognize its first beginnings and so know how to avoid putting obstacles in the way of what the Holy Spirit wants to bestow on them. (See also SSD, p. 181.)

What contemplative prayer is not

Before we sketch briefly what our deepening immersion in the Trinity is, we must insist that it is very far from an oriental state of impersonal awareness produced by techniques and methods. Thus it should not be confused with Buddhist or Hindu exercises. Nor is it introspection, dwelling on one's own inner life, feelings, and thoughts. And of course, we are not here speaking about visions and revelations—these are not meant for everyone. Finally, our contemplation is not simply thinking things over. Nor is it more or less strong emotional feelings about God and religious matters. (See also FW, pp. 7, 57; SSD, pp. 69, 83–84, 135–36, 156–59, 171.)

What contemplation is

While meditative prayer involves reading, thinking, imagining, drawing conclusions, and conversing inwardly with the indwelling Trinity, contemplation is none of these things. Rather it is a real awareness of God, desiring and loving him, which we do not produce but simply receive from him when we are ready for it. There are no images, ideas, or words. In the first stages what he gives is usually a dry desire for him (that is, with little or no feelings), or it is a gentle, delightful awareness of his presence. Both of these two types of awareness are brief. They are "just there", that is, not produced in a human manner. They cannot be had whenever we want them. No methods or techniques can produce them. When we have lived the Gospel generously in our state in life—and this includes fidelity to meditative prayer—God begins to grant this superior type of communing with himself.

What the Lord gives ("infuses" is another word for this) is at first usually delicate, gentle, and brief. The recipient will most likely continue to experience distractions. But this advancing type of prayer progressively grows as time goes on in both depth and duration—again we repeat, *if* we continue to live the gospel in a wholehearted manner. At times it can become a deep absorption, so deep that distractions cease for five or ten minutes. However, this absorbing prayer is advancing contemplation, which we need not explain further at this point. (For more, however, see FW, pp. 57–71, 86–107; SSD, pp. 154–59, 267–78; CCC 2709–19.)

Transition from meditation to contemplation

Living things, we have noted, develop gradually, not by leaps and bounds. Each of us has spent nine months in his mother's womb, then several years as an infant and child, more years as teenager and young adult. Then comes middle age and maturity. So also our communing with God is a gradual process from the humanly produced kind of relationship to the divinely given desiring and loving. This latter itself grows in depth and splendor all the way to what is called the transforming union. (See FW, pp. 175–97.) This growth process "from one glory to another" (2 Cor 3:18) is due to the divine initiative, not to our mere wish to have it happen. The transition stage is part of the gradual growth to a fullness.

Marvelous though created realities are, they cannot of

themselves lead us to deep intimacy with Father, Son, and Holy Spirit. There is no human power that can bring us into the inner trinitarian life. Something radically new is needed. In a similar way, human muscle power, even that of the most gifted athlete, will never be enough for anyone to jump to the moon. Something basically different is needed: rocket power.

God is not only greater than anything created: he is endlessly greater. He is purest and unlimited power . . . love . . . joy . . . goodness . . . life . . . beauty. Literally he is unspeakable. That we may know and embrace him intimately he must take the initiative to bridge the endless gap. He alone can do it. He must bestow the new light, love, beauty, delight. Since we are not talking now about visions or revelations, it is a question of a new kind of prayer beyond all created input, images, ideas. It is a divine way of praying, far beyond our human capacities. How is this infinite gap bridged?

The Lord alone does it when we are ready. And beginners get ready by daily meditative prayer together with getting rid of their venial sins. When they are sufficiently purified by this renewing lifestyle, they will begin to notice on occasion an inclination at prayer to leave thinking aside. At the same time they notice a desire to be with God in a wordless way. At other times they will be inclined to meditate. They are in the transitional stage.

The rule of thumb at this point is to follow the lead of the Holy Spirit, that is, you do what he inclines you to do at prayer time. If you find it easy to meditate and it seems to work, then do that. If, on the other hand, you are inclined simply to be with him without words, do that. Be patient during this transition period. Do not worry about occasional, unwilled distractions that occur. Be gentle in turning away from them and back to the Lord who is drawing you. (For more, see FW, pp. 54–55, 86–87; SSD, pp. 183–90.)

Degrees of growth

Like our examples of the acorn becoming the oak or the baby developing into the teenager and the adult, contemplative communion with the Trinity gradually grows in both duration and intensity—as long as the person remains self-giving in the usual details of human life. One slowly leaves the transitional stage as the infused desire and love for the Lord becomes habitual. If all goes well, once in a while there may be a profound and intensely delightful absorption in God, when for a few minutes there are no distractions at all. If one continues to grow, this communion can become ecstatic and then should grow on to the summit, the transforming union. These advanced degrees of contemplation are described in FW, pp. 57–71. Sts. Teresa of Avila and John of the Cross explain them at length and with details and sublime beauty.

Scripture proclaims contemplation for everyone

For some strange reason not easy to fathom, many religiously minded men and women seem not to realize how frequently and strongly the biblical word speaks of this remarkable intimacy each of us is called to have with our unspeakable God. It is an interpersonal closeness, identical with what we are discussing so briefly in this chapter. Scripture couches this intimacy in expressions of touching beauty, loveliness, charm—and, yes, tenderness. Some illustrations will help.

We are to "look to the Lord and be radiant with joy . . . to taste and experience" how surpassingly good he is (Ps 34:5, 8). This communing with him is the most important thing we are privileged to do in our lives: "to gaze on the divine beauty", a perfect definition of contemplative prayer (Ps 27:4). We are invited to grow to the point where our mind's eye is on him always (Ps 25:15), that is, to be head over heels in love with our Origin and our unspeakable Destiny—which, of course, makes us all the better for everyone else. This constant divine awareness is one of the traits of the transforming summit. Not surprisingly our "very heart and our flesh sing for joy to the living God" (Ps 84:2). We hunger and thirst for him after the manner of a parched desert needing the refreshment of clear, cool water (Ps 63:1).

The New Testament continues and deepens the message of the old dispensation. We who hunger and thirst for quenching at the unlimited Fountain (Is 55:1–3; Rev 22:17; Jn 7:37–39) are to be filled with his utter fullness, a mind-boggling thought (Eph 3:19–20). We are called to be overflowing with his "inexpressible joy", to be "rejoicing always", to be "praying always and everywhere" (1 Pet 1:8; Phil 4:4; Lk 18:1). We are to give thanks and praise to our Lord in everything we do (Col 3:15, 17). How more exalted could the human person be? Indeed, eye has not seen, ear has not heard, we cannot even dream of what God has in store for those who love him (1 Cor 2:9).

Because Sacred Scripture is written for people in all states of life, all of these contemplative texts express the goal for all of us, beginners as well as the advanced. It goes without saying that the teachings of the Church and her saints through the centuries have the same clear message as what the inspired word declares. She places these very texts, and others like them, on our lips repeatedly in her official liturgies. (See also FW, pp. 202–16; SSD, pp. 176–78.)

Transformation of daily life

Even though contemplative prayer does not usually suggest specific solutions to the ordinary problems of daily life, it does go a long way in providing an insightful atmosphere and a mighty motivation to address them with love. As husband and wife grow in their intimacy with God, loving dialogue and listening to each other tend to replace arguing and bickering. They become more inclined to compromise in practicalities, that is, when no principle is at stake. A genuine love for each other and for their children necessarily deepens. A conviction arises that unity and a shared vision take precedence over the attitude that "I must have my way." A joyous willingness to embrace sacrifices and hardships replaces complaining and bitterness. The spouses generously forgive each other and seek forgiveness for their own faults. With the growing divine light and love, which lie at the very core of contemplative prayer, they see things with perspective and proportion: big things appear big and trivial things trivial. They become more real, seeing reality as it actually is. It is easy to see why marriages in which both partners are committed to a deep prayer life are happy indeed. If all this appears utopian, I can only say: Try it out and you will see.

All this is true, obviously, for convents and rectories, nursing homes and hospitals—indeed for all primary communities. Contemplative clergy, for example, are more concerned and compassionate and caring at the bedside and in the confessional. Their homilies, stemming as they do from inner fire, are far more effective and have greater impact. This is why saints in all states of life change not only themselves; they change the world as well—at least that part of the world willing to give up its egocentrism.

Meditation developing slowly into contemplation transforms people from the inside out. Men and women come alive with a renewing joy and inner vibrancy as they leave aside the artificial stimulations of worldliness and shed the boredom and jadedness worldly trivialities bring about. As they turn to triune Beauty in a progressively deepening prayer life, their inner empty aching is replaced by experiencing what eye has not seen, nor ear heard: a transformation from one glory to another (2 Cor 3:18).

PART THREE

CHURCH AND FAMILY

Liturgical Prayer

It is safe to say that when most people think of prayer they do not first of all imagine ceremonies, priests, and incense. Novices have much to learn before they give much thought to official gatherings in a cathedral or a parish church. So once again we ask, why this chapter?

First of all, deep in every human heart is a need to worship and to thank. One of the frustrations the atheist has to face (as Chesterton pointed out) is to experience the innocence of a baby's face or the splendor of a nighttime sky and then have no one to thank for it. And because we are social beings, we need on occasion to express this gratitude and adoration together with other people. We need liturgy.

Secondly, the first Christians understood this radical human need, for they came together with one heart and soul to celebrate the Eucharist (which means thanksgiving) in community, to listen to the proclaimed word and to share other prayers as well (Acts 2:42; 4:31–32). They are models for us. They knew themselves to be a society of prayer, a corporate priesthood of praise (1 Pet 2:9).

They rejoiced to be a people of great joy in their gatherings for worship (1 Pet 1:8; Phil 4:4, 6).

Thirdly, the Church today is of the same mind. It is for our own good that she requires us to participate together in Sunday Mass, and she encourages this on a daily basis for those who can find the time. When Pope Paul VI introduced to the whole Church the revised Liturgy of the Hours, he explicitly declared that "the Hours are recommended to all Christ's faithful members" (LC, no. 8). All! How could a faithful prayer primer fail to further this recommendation, especially when one sees the reasons for it?

Fourthly, the Church's liturgy is itself a splendid teacher of the what and how of prayer. Made up mainly of the inspired biblical word, this official worship instructs us in the divine manner of communing with the Father, the Son, and the Holy Spirit. Beginners need to be immersed in this indispensable divine fountain and crystal mirror.

Lastly, we include this chapter in our primer because the sacramental power of the liturgy nourishes our prayer in all of its stages of growth from private vocal communing, through meditative pondering, and on to the very heights of burning contemplative love.

Communal prayer

The liturgy is obviously a community activity, and as such it enjoys a special favor of the Lord: Where two or three are gathered together in his name, he takes up a new presence among them (Mt 18:20). The early Church understood the message. After Jesus' ascension into heaven, the apostles knew that their first duty was not to get on the road for the work of proclaiming the message, but to "join in continuous prayer together with several women, including Mary the mother of Jesus, and with his brothers" (Acts 1:14, JB). Only then, after their long forty-day retreat and the coming of the Holy Spirit, were they fitted to do their work well. Later, when a persecution began, the faithful again lifted their voices to God and were powerfully "filled with the Holy Spirit" (Acts 4:24, 31, see also Acts 12:5, 12). Their prayer in common led them to continue individually in singing and chanting to the Lord in their hearts—even in the midst of their work activities.

Communal prayer, therefore, is not merely a luxury. It stems from the very nature of the Church, the Lord's own family. While we must go to the Father regularly in individual solitude (Mt 6:6; Lk 5:16), we also pursue him as communities in our families, our parishes, in convents and monasteries.

What is liturgical prayer?

Our Catholic liturgy is the communal and official worship of the Church Jesus founded to teach, sanctify, and govern in his name: "Go into the whole world, make disciples and teach . . . I am with you always, even to the end of time. . . . He who hears you, hears me" (Mt 28:18–20; Lk 10:16).

Part of this divine commission is to organize our communal worship, to enrich and beautify it through the centuries, and to preserve both words and ceremonies

pure from errors and exaggerated extremes. Because the
Church is the bride of Christ (2 Cor 11:2), her public and
official worship becomes, as we have already noted, the
"voice of the bride singing to her Spouse" (SC, no. 84).
It would be difficult to express more splendidly what we
do in our churches and chapels when we gather together
for prayer.

Mass, the daily summit

Participation in the Eucharistic sacrifice is the highest of
all our prayers, and most effectively when contemplative
love burns in the hearts of the celebrant and the laity
alike. Why is the Mass so sublime? It is the unbloody re-
offering of the paschal mystery: the passion, death, and
Resurrection of Jesus himself, the Supreme Priest, both
victim and victor.

The Lord once said to Angela of Foligno "Make yourself a capacity, and I will make myself a torrent." The
Eucharist is indeed a cascade of power, love, and beauty.
To drink deeply of this torrent we need to mature as persons, to give up self-centered clinging to our sins and their
deadening burdens. As these obstacles are removed, we
gradually drink more and more of the rushing waters of
the liturgy and imbibe their refreshing light and delight.

This is why the saints without exception love the Eucharist so much and why those who imitate them closely
go to daily Mass when it is at all possible in their state
in life. These people, alive to the word of God and its
power, notice carefully and ponder the texts of the liturgy,

most of which are directly from Scripture itself. Even the prayers the Church herself has composed allude to the biblical message, explain its meaning, and apply it to our lives.

Here also is one reason among others why saintly men and women in all vocations love their contemplative prayer both as precious in itself and also as providing the inner element of their liturgical worship. They rightly see this Holy Sacrifice as the very peak of each day. For a rich explanation of the central and irreplaceable place of the Eucharist in our lives, see CCC 1322–1405.

Are you enthusiastic?

But not everyone is a saint. One of the most common excuses we hear from people who are tepid about attending Mass, who easily and with little or no regret omit their Sunday obligation, is the complaint that "it's not meaningful to me; I don't get anything out of it; I find it boring." These alleged reasons are not considered by the one complaining to be defects in himself. Rather they are conceived as something wrong with the Eucharistic Sacrifice itself.

Before we respond to this thinking (or better, lack of thinking) let me grant that sadly enough there are priests who disregard the Church's norms for a beautiful, dignified, reverent celebration of Mass. Some of these, and others as well, present homilies that are sprinkled with platitudes and private opinions with little doctrinal content. Yes, there are also those who lack public-speaking abilities and whose ideas are not clearly explained and illustrated. It is true likewise that some seem not to be on fire themselves.

Yet at the same time there are other priests who are faithful, obedient, and talented. The clergy are not the main cause of the alleged boredom. If your parish priest is an obstacle, then find a normal situation. We take the trouble to shop around for other things we really want and consider important.

What then is the core of the boredom problem? It is the same as with most kinds of tedium. Monotony is due chiefly to the spiritual poverty of bored people. They are so poor in human development that they are more or less insensitive to seeing and appreciating beauty lying right before their eyes. They can read Shakespeare and listen to Mozart without being thrilled or the least moved by what well-rounded men and women find stimulating and exciting. The awesome wonders of creation (an atom, a tiny living cell, galaxies of billions of immense stars, a psalm verse) leave them cold and unimpressed. They are partially or totally deaf in mind and heart.

Why, then, are some people unimpressed at Mass? Their instruction in the faith may have been close to nil. Or they have been so given to the artificial tinsel of worldliness and/or deliberate sin that they are inwardly dulled or dead to genuine splendor. People who profess to get nothing from a Beethoven symphony or from an article dealing with a recent discovery in microbiology are saying far more about themselves than about the music or the science. So also our liturgical worship. In plain

English: People who say they get little from Mass are those who bring little. They are toddlers who have a lot of growing to do.

Psalms in the liturgy

Among all the books of prayer the psalms enjoy a unique place. For one thing, they are divinely inspired, God's own word. They have also enjoyed a privileged position in both esteem and practice through the centuries-old history of God's people, New Testament as well as Old. Because I am writing here for beginners, I shall not attempt an extensive introduction to the psalter. This can be found both in specialized books and introductions to the psalms in large biblical commentaries.

Rather I shall explain why these inspired prayers are so prominent and moving in our liturgies. First of all, they express our universal human needs as do no other prayers. They enthusiastically invite us to rejoice in all of God's wonders, one by one; to exult in him and dance for joy (for example, Ps 9:1–2). They put touching sentiments of sorrow in our hearts and on our lips: pleading for divine mercy and tenderness as the Lord wipes away our faults and as we are purified of our guilt (for example, Ps 51:1–2). Just as we all need to wonder joyously in the divine marvels and to ask for God's loving healing, so the psalms express charmingly our thirsting for the divine Fountain who alone can quench our longing for him and cure our wounds (for example, Ps 63:1–2). To these illustrations of our universal needs we could add others: the necessity we experience to love fully and passionately, to praise unending Beauty, to make the Lord our consuming joy and the sole rest of our souls.

The second reason the psalms are so apt for liturgical worship is that they provide us with a host of images that we in our technological and machine-driven societies so desperately need: clapping forests, towering clouds, streams and mountains, dancing maidens, everyone singing for sheer joy. These divinely inspired songs incarnate our prayer needs in expressions far richer than we would or could imagine if left to our own resources.

Thirdly, the divine words of Scripture place on our lips and in our minds thoughts of interpersonal intimacy with the awesome God of the galaxies that, left to ourselves, we would not dare to conceive or utter: ardent thirsting, loving, adoring, tasting. We are invited to gaze on the unlimited loveliness of the Lord, expecting all of our noblest desires to be fulfilled. One could go on and on.

Because the psalms are so prominent both at Mass and especially in the Liturgy of the Hours, it is good to recall that we are praying not only in our own names but also in the name of the universal Church spread throughout the world. On one occasion we personally may feel sad while the psalmist (and many of the faithful spread over the earth) are shouting and dancing for joy. On another occasion we may be bursting with wonderment and delight while the particular psalm has us calling to the Lord from the depths of sorrow, sin, and pain. Pertinent here is St. Paul's admonition that we "rejoice with those who rejoice and be sad with those in sorrow" (Rom 12:15).

Likewise on many feastdays (such as Christmas, Easter,

Corpus Christi, Assumption) psalms are chosen because of their christological, messianic, and Marian meanings and applications (GILH, nos. 108–9). Again we are praying in union with the whole Mystical Body of the Lord and voicing its sentiments and aspirations.

Liturgical prayer is personally precious

For a number of reasons the official worship of the Church promotes our own individual spiritual lives. One reason is, as we have already noted, that most of our liturgical texts are directly from the inspired Scriptures. Consequently, while they are communal, they enrich the individual as well. God made us to be both social and individual persons. We need to communicate with him and be nourished in both manners.

Another reason is that even the prayers that the Church composes often refer to, or are partially derived from, biblical sources, and hence they share in the impact deriving from the Lord's love and truth.

A third importance of liturgical worship is that through the celebration of the hours we sanctify the various times of our days and nights together with all their activities, joys and sufferings, successes and failures. We likewise prepare ourselves for the next celebration of Mass.

Even more: in liturgical worship we join with the heavenly Church in eternally singing her praises and thanksgiving to the Lord of glory, Father, Son, and Holy Spirit (Rev 8:2–4; SC, no. 83). We are reminded, too, by the formula at the end of many prayers, ". . . through our Lord Jesus Christ . . .", that we are in union with our risen High Priest in offering adoration, praise, petition, and love to the eternal Father (Heb 7:23–25; GILH, no. 17).

For all these reasons we are not surprised that the Church throughout the world invites laymen and women to join the clergy and religious in celebrating all of her official worship both at Mass and in the Liturgy of the Hours. (See GILH 21–23, 26–27. Consult especially the extended treatment in CCC 1076–1109 and 1136–73.)

I I

Liturgy of the Hours

Much like our chapter on contemplation, this present one would not rank high on a list of what most people would expect in a book for beginners. Yet I trust that as we proceed it will become clear that to exclude it would be seriously to shortchange you, the reader. Why? It is safe to say that you want not only to begin to pray but also to advance. No one begins a trip to travel only ten percent of the way. You want both a full personal prayer life and a vibrant sharing in the Church's pilgrimage to the Father, with his Son, and through their Holy Spirit.

Throughout the centuries the Church has rejoiced to sing to her Lord in her official prayer, the Liturgy of the Hours—also called the divine office or the breviary. Through all these ages priests and many religious have had the happy duty to sing or recite this prayer during certain hours of the day and night, every day of the year, in the name of and for God's people. Today the laity are invited to join the clergy, either privately alone at home or in groups, in celebrating this liturgical communing with God. All of us are reminded in the book of Revelation to sing or recite the praises of the Blessed Trinity in union with the heavenly choirs of angels and saints (Rev 8:2–4). And all of us are urged to pray in union with the risen Jesus, who lives forever to intercede for all who go to the Father through him (Heb 7:25). This is ecclesial prayer, that is, the prayer of the *ecclesia*, the Church the Lord himself established.

Just what is the Liturgy of the Hours?

This divine office is the Catholic Church's loving and powerful adoration, praise, and worship of the Blessed Trinity in all the mysteries of creation and in the beautiful deeds of salvation history together with the eternal ecstasy of the beatific vision of the saints. This glorious panorama is presented to us in a continuing celebration unlimited in all directions throughout the liturgical year. We not only see this unfolding drama as spectators. We share in it and are immersed in it both in the Eucharistic Sacrifice and in the Liturgy of the Hours. We deal with the latter in this chapter.

The contents of this official prayer book are derived mainly from the inspired Scriptures of both Testaments. Included also are excerpts from the writings of the Church's most gifted luminaries through twenty centuries: her saints, poets, literary figures, Scripture scholars, and theologians (most of the latter are also saints). Liturgical specialists in recent decades have worked under the guidance of leadership in the Church to arrange competently and artistically selections from all these sources into the coherent whole we admire and use today. These two intimately intertwined fountains of Scripture and tradition explain the unique taste, fragrance, charm, and power of the Liturgy of the Hours.

Thus the hymns, psalms, antiphons, readings, and prayers are chosen and composed to explain and celebrate the seasons and feasts as they unfold throughout each year. These combine to present and aid us in reliving the principal events in and the stages of salvation history. There are also, of course, many linkages interwoven between the Liturgy of the Hours and the daily Eucharistic Sacrifice—not only in texts but also in the deep contemplative love that burns in the faithful ones who celebrate both of them.

Expressing this enrichment

The spiritual wealth of the Liturgy of the Hours cannot be expressed in a single sentence or paragraph. Thus for the sake of both clarity and brevity we shall distinguish a number of ways of explaining this lush superabundance. The celebration of this public prayer of the universal Church is at one and same time

—the united prayer of God's people throughout the world and thus is never-ending in each successive time zone, we as her members in a flowing continuity praise, worship, love, and petition the Father, through his Son and in their Holy Spirit;

—a hymn of praise that Jesus' community has been singing through the centuries; we join the angels and the saints, our ancestors and companions, in their eternal rejoicing in our triune God;

—a divine-human dialogue in which "God speaks to his people [in his inspired word and through the Church he founded to do this], and his people reply to him in song and prayer" (SC, no. 33);

—a worldwide celebration of trinitarian truth, goodness, and beauty; joining with the heavenly choir in its delightful immersion in divine Beauty (Rev 5:9; 7:9–12; 8:2–4; SC, no. 83; LG, no. 50);

—a means of sanctifying the whole day: morning, midday, afternoon, evening and night—and even the middle of the night for those who offer the office of readings then;

—an organized communal prayer celebrated with the leadership of a priest, or by members of a religious community, or by individuals in any state of life; in differing ways all these participate in the official worship of the Mystical Body spread throughout our global village;

—an overflow from the endless riches of the Eucharistic Sacrifice we have just celebrated and a preparation for the wealth of tomorrow's Mass;

—the voice of Jesus himself praying in and for each one of us and for all of us together.

Historical enrichments

Besides being rooted in the inspired Scriptures, the divine office has gradually been formed, enlarged, and enriched through the centuries. Popes, poets, biblical scholars, gifted theologians, and saints on fire have shared their love and their talents for the nourishment of all the faithful.

In our own day Pius XII undertook the updating work of liturgical revision, the principles of which were formulated by Vatican Council II. Pope Paul VI remarked that this conciliar enterprise was carried through "with such thoroughness and skill, such spirituality and power, that there is scarcely a parallel to it in the entire history of the Church" (LC, p. 13).

The actual production of our new revision in all its details and wealth was the result of seven years of work by scholars in the liturgical, biblical, theological, spiritual, and pastoral fields. After a worldwide consultation of bishops, pastors, religious, and laity, the new Liturgy of the Hours was approved by the Holy Father for the universal Church. For a brief but beautiful explanation of this official prayer, see CCC 1174-78.

Meant for all the faithful

Because the New Testament itself defines the Church as a royal priesthood of praise (1 Pet 2:9), it is no surprise that the Holy See has repeatedly recommended the divine office to all the faithful members of Christ (LC, no. 8). Because this matter is so important, priests are expressly admonished to "see to it that the faithful are invited—and prepared by suitable instruction—to celebrate the principal Hours in common, especially on Sundays and feast days. They should teach them how to make the celebration a sincere prayer; they should therefore give them suitable guidance in the Christian understanding of the psalms, so that they may be led by degrees to a greater appreciation and more frequent use of the prayer of the Church" (GILH, no. 23).

There are many varied settings and circumstances in which all members in the various states in life can participate in being the Church at prayer before daily Mass in the local parish, in each home, in neighborhood meetings, at a convent or rectory or nursing home gathering, in family reunions, during anniversary celebrations. It is significant that the ordinary family of husband, wife, and children is worthy of special mention by the Vatican. The Congregation of Divine Worship in its document on the Liturgy of the Hours states that it is "desirable that the family, the domestic sanctuary of the Church, should not only pray together to God but should also celebrate some parts of the Liturgy of the Hours as occasion offers, so as to enter more deeply into the life of the Church" (GILH, no. 27).

Yes, indeed, "where two or three are gathered in my name, there I am in their midst" (Mt 18:20).

Learning the Liturgy of the Hours

At this point in our discussion one might say, "Yes, this divine office is beautiful, and I'd like to take it up, but isn't it also hard to learn? It seems pretty complicated, and we lay people have no special training." The answer to this question is both Yes and No. Yes, it does take some time and practice to "get the drift", to attain an ease in celebrating the various hours and feasts and seasons. But this is true of any number of worthy accomplishments: baking bread, playing the violin, driving a car, learning to use a word processor. But no, learning this prayer of the Church is not nearly as complex as playing a musical instrument or becoming adept with a computer or mastering the rudiments of biology. Many new skills can seem forbidding at first, but with some help, instruction, and a bit of patience they soon become easy enough.

How would you learn the Liturgy of the Hours? A friend, a priest, a religious can offer guidance with no great expenditure of time. As I write this paragraph the thought flashes into my mind of a flight from New York to London. I sat next to a Mormon youth, and after we had a pleasant chat for about an hour on matters religious, I took out my Liturgy of the Hours to offer the office of readings. He was inquisitive, and so I explained the general idea of it by going through the hefty volume with him. He was fascinated that such a prayer book even existed. He seemed more interested in those ten minutes of explanation than in anything else I had said in an hour.

But back to answering the question interrupted by the flashing thought . . . In addition to the help another person can offer you, instructional materials (a booklet or pamphlet) should be available at Catholic bookstores. You will find some directions in the text itself. Joining a parish group and learning by participating with others can be a pleasant and smooth introduction to this mine of devotion and personal growth.

Hints for celebrating well

Because the psalms have so prominent a place within the divine office, ones does well to seek a better scriptural formation and understanding of them by instruction and personal study—in accord, of course, with one's own individual capacities. Meditation on these inspired prayers verse by verse will enhance one's grasp, taste, and appreciation for them. A growing daily personal enrichment naturally follows.

By their character the psalms are poetic and musical. They are songs even when we recite them. They are likewise aimed mainly at moving hearts and wills (GILH, nos. 103–4). Therefore, whether we recite or sing them, our spirit should be vibrant, loving, and joyful. We are a celebrating people, rejoicing in the Lord always (Phil 4:4).

Even though the Liturgy of the Hours can profoundly nourish the individual person, we recall that we are praying in the name of the universal Temple of the Spirit, which is the Church. We therefore open our minds and hearts to this ecclesial dimension especially "when a psalm of joy confronts a person who is sad and overcome with grief, or a psalm of sorrow confronts a person full of joy" (GILH, no. 108). When we pray with the universal Church our vision and our love are both expanded. We become more authentic.

Each part of the divine office has its specific purposes.

For example, the longer instructional texts in the office of readings are meant to enlighten, move, and nourish our spiritual lives from the treasures of Scripture, the early patristic giants, and other outstanding witnesses to the Church's centuries-old patrimony (GILH, no. 165). The shorter biblical reading in each of the daily hours is a short scriptural gem of a few sentences, ideally suited for further prayerful pondering.

The responsories that follow these texts are meant to throw further light on them and thus to foster their inner meaningfulness in our lives with the Lord and one another (GILH, no. 169).

The hymns that begin each of the daily hours immediately incite divine praise, and they create the spirit of the hour or of the individual feast. Whether these hymns are sung or recited, they also move our hearts by the beauty of their sentiments, thought content, and poetic style (GILH, no. 173).

As the chief of all prayers, we say the Our Father three times in our daily liturgies: once during Mass, once during morning prayer, and once at evening prayer. In keeping with its dignity as coming from the heart and lips of Jesus himself, the Church wishes us to join together frequently in celebrating his words and sentiments in their awesome depth.

Our ecclesial guidelines for the renewed liturgy recommend brief times of prayerful silence within the celebration of both the Eucharist and the office. These pauses usually occur after the readings, the homily (at Mass), and the psalms. Their purpose is to provide brief times when we may inwardly converse with the Lord and fix his words more deeply in our minds and hearts (SC, no. 30; GILH, nos. 201–3).

The Liturgy of the Hours: A jewel

The simple fact that we are dealing with the official prayer of the Church, Jesus' spouse whom he cherishes with an entirely special love (Eph 5:25–26), necessarily gives it a unique value. We have noted above that this prayer extends our concerns to the needs of our brothers and sisters everywhere. The intercessions at morning and evening prayers teach us to widen our thoughts and petitions beyond the limits of our own immediate family, friendships, city, and nation. Without neglecting our naturally close and dear ones, we are reminded that we have other multitudes to cherish and aid.

In this one worldwide people of God, who live in all time zones, time itself is consecrated in our one communal prayer life. This spouse of Christ is literally "praying at all times, never losing heart" (Lk 18:1). From the rising of the sun to its setting, in a continuous movement from east to west, we glory in sharing in the never-ending love for and adoration of our triune God, offering through Jesus "an unceasing sacrifice of praise" (Heb 13:15).

As a further blessing the divine office feeds and nourishes our private vocal, meditative, and contemplative prayer lives both by its texts and in its periods of silence —just as in the reverse direction our private prayer nourishes our liturgical life. Again we note that truth makes one beautiful whole.

Like everything else, but in special ways, the Liturgy of the Hours flows from and to the very summit of the divine economy of salvation: the paschal mystery we celebrate in the Eucharistic Sacrifice. With divinely inspired words it prepares our minds and hearts for celebrating this renewal of Jesus' death and Resurrection. It deepens our participation as we drink of this inexhaustible fountain-head of all grace. Thus this official prayer of the Mystical Body is the ideal preparation for "the center and summit of the whole life of the Christian community", which is the Mass itself (CD, no. 30).

The place of the Liturgy of the Hours in everyone's journey to God is well summarized by the teaching Church herself. Referring to the magnificent renewal of this official prayer, Pope Paul VI declared as he promulgated it that "it is supremely to be hoped that the Liturgy of the Hours may pervade and penetrate the whole of Christian prayer, giving it life, direction and expression, and effectively nourishing the spiritual life of the people of God" (LC, no. 8).

12

Family Prayer

Now we share a secret: there are two audiences for this prayer primer. One is obviously not hidden at all. These are adults and teenagers who have come to the conclusion that this world is simply not enough—it just cannot satisfy their deepest longings. They therefore want a vibrant relationship with God, the number one priority in any sensible person's life. They seek help in this pursuit, and they want to know how to begin it.

The second audience is totally unaware of this radical need, even though they also share it: small children, so small they cannot read these pages. How can they receive the message? Either through their parents who are reading these lines, or perhaps through their teachers at school or through people who run day-care centers.

The ideal and divinely planned setting for introducing young children to a loving relationship with God is a happily married mother and father who themselves have a growing prayer life (CCC 2226). When they take suitable steps to share it with their offspring, great things can happen. Hence, we entitle this chapter "Family Prayer". But we urge anyone who is privileged to work with children to adapt what we say here to other circumstances. These include single parents, kindergartens, ordinary schools, catechism classes, day-care centers. All that is needed is good will, some knowledge of prayer, and a lively imagination. Yes, of course, we assume that we relate to the youngsters with thought patterns and language suitable to their ages.

The domestic church

A happy home has been called "the domestic sanctuary of the Church" (see our preceding chapter). A normal family, which is of course a family in a serious pursuit of God, provides the first setting and atmosphere for children to meet their Lord. A refreshing openness to the divine is one of the core traits of youngsters so praised by Jesus himself, traits that we adults must also have as a condition for entering the kingdom (Mt 18:1–4).

If from their earliest days infants see Mom and Dad praying, they rightly assume that prayer is as normal as having dinner together. If parents hold them on their laps or at their sides as they commune with the Lord before bedtime, the youngsters learn even without explicit words to that effect that prayer is pleasant, perhaps even a fun thing to do. We are thinking here not only of vocal prayer, which the children may simply listen to at first, but also of meditative prayer, which on occasion the parents may verbalize in simple terms. More of this shortly. (See CCC 2685.)

The atmosphere

Just as in a convent or monastery, a prayerful atmosphere is one that is penetrated with love for God and for others, so also in the marriage community. A milieu conducive to prayer happens when Mother and Father are convinced that the two greatest commandments are top priority in their home (CCC 2223). All through the nitty gritty of each day, and week after week, they are at pains to be gentle toward each other and toward the children. Firmness with the children on occasion, yes, but a loving and patient firmness. No harsh words, no nagging, no raising of voices, no quarreling—and generous forgiveness when there is a slip.

Why is this gentle tone so important for anyone's prayer life? The reason is basic and simple: Prayer itself is obviously a love matter. This primer is full of the idea. If there is conflict or harshness in the routine of daily life, all of us (children included) find incongruity, if not pain, in trying to shift gears into something as sublime as conversing with the Lord. If, on the other hand, genuine harmony and esteem for one another penetrate our habitual interpersonal relationships on the human level, turning to commune with God on the divine level is smooth and normal.

Pre-formation of children for prayer

The healthy, unspoiled child is typically full of life—which is why two- or three-year-olds are more inclined to run than to walk, why some are almost constantly in motion. Closely allied with this trait is their readiness to question and wonder, especially if parents and teachers take the trouble to point out the numberless marvels in all of creation (see EPB, Chapters 7–10). For example, it takes almost no time to explain and discuss the vein system of a single leaf and what is happening in it, and in every other leaf on this tree—right now. Or for a little older child: "How long do you think it would take a jet plane traveling at five hundred miles per hour to reach the sun?" (Do your homework before you try that question—you may be amazed yourself.) "Why does the moon seem to accompany us as we drive in the country at night? Why can you wiggle your toes just by wanting to wiggle them?" There is no end to examples that can excite wonder in normal children, or in any adult who is still intellectually alive.

As a preparation for meditative prayer parents and teachers should also introduce children to the appreciation of beauty. How? Just invite them to gaze quietly at a sunset for a minute or two in silence and then talk with them about it. How big is the sun? How far away is it? How long does it take the sunlight to get to earth? Do we see the sun where exactly it is right now? Or ponder together a tree or flower or carrot or radish. Or study together in a science book or encyclopedia the wonder of a bird's wing. Later on marvel with your offspring about atoms, molecules, living cells, the solar system, our galaxy, the entire universe. You and they come alive. Take the time. This enrichment of your children is more important than eating lunch. If you wish a readily available source for material on wonders like these, see the EPB reference above.

Now what does this all have to do with prayer? A great deal. It is a short step from experiencing wonder, amazement and beauty to praising, thanking, and loving the supreme Artist of it all, who is endless Beauty. See our chapter 5 to be reminded again of how expressive the psalter is in making this very point and how abundantly it illustrates what we are saying here.

Beginning with vocal prayer

We get to know people personally by communicating with them: a greeting, a smile, a nod, but mostly by speaking and listening and responding. Babies learn words and phrases from parents and siblings, but as they develop they begin to conceive their own ideas and ways to express them. Prayer is communicating with God, and little tots begin by using the vocal prayers they hear and are taught. But as they develop they can learn to express their own thoughts in their own words—even though they continue to use formulas such as the Our Father, the Hail Mary, and the Glory Be . . .

In teaching vocal prayers we should accustom children to pray at a reasonable pace, "not rattling as the pagans do" (Mt 6:7). This lets them know that we take seriously these conversations with God, his Mother, and the saints. This deliberateness likewise promotes attending with our minds to what we are saying with our lips.

Once in a while, especially at the beginning of learning vocal prayers, it is good to explain to the youngsters one word or phrase of the prayer before reciting it. For example, "Father" or "kingdom". These explanations should not be offered too often, so as not to interrupt prayer time unduly or to create a burden for young minds and hearts.

As time goes on parents and teachers introduce their charges to formulating their own vocal prayers, while they continue with the memorized ones. This prepares them for more personal intimacy with the Lord and his saints, and of course for meditative prayer as well.

Teaching meditation to children

Because of the very nature of the family, parents are the first educators of their children (CCC 2223). At the top of the list of their formational duties are those that deal with the supernatural welfare of their offspring. Much of what this primer contains can be successfully taught to young children and teenagers. As any skilled teacher knows, instruction must be couched in vocabulary and imaginative thought patterns suited to the age and development of the pupils. Perhaps some day a mother or father or teacher may, alone or together, write a prayer primer for tots and those who teach them.

How precisely might we teach small children to meditate? Abstract explanations will not get us very far. The concrete verbalizing of a short meditation would seem the way to go. For example, we might say something like the following: "Now close your eyes because we are going to think about God living inside us, and then talk quietly to him. He is everywhere, and he is in your heart. Right now. (Pause) And he loves you much, much more than you love yourself. (Pause) Lord, I love you too. (Pause)

Wow, you are really something! (Pause) You made me, you love me so much. (Pause) How can I thank you enough? (Pause) Help me to think of you more often. I adore you and praise you. You made the whole earth and every big and little flower. (Pause) I love you. Goodbye for now." For little tots these initial sessions of learning by doing should be short and simple. Their attention spans are brief. It goes without saying that source materials for reflections abound in Scripture, *The Imitation of Christ*, and in other classics. But they must be put into simple terms.

A family project

Meditative prayer can become a family enterprise, though most people would hardly imagine the idea, let alone the reality. We are all familiar with communal prayer before and after meals, in reciting the rosary, and other prayers, morning and evening. But it is good to know that there are married couples who silently commune with God in contemplative prayer, either alone or together. In an ideal home it can happen as easily as turning on the television set.

Meditation can occur with children participating as well. With permission I will share the experience of a friend who is also a spiritual director:

> I was deeply touched recently by a young mother who had great difficulty in finding a time she could spend in prayer. . . . No wonder, . . . she has four children in grade school! She decided to incorporate her whole family. They use HANDOUT No. 1 [given to the mother by this spiritual

director] as their meditation guide for a particular Scripture. The entire family participates in the reading, discussion, and prayer after their evening meal. She said it works beautifully. The participation, and insight the children share is profound. The Lord helps her "to carry this over" into her own time of quiet before she goes to bed. I was so blessed by this—to see a family learning and growing together in Jesus!

Where there is a will (and imagination) there is a way.

The same is true, as we have already indicated in chapter 11, of the Liturgy of the Hours. The official Church, as the bride of Christ, herself warmly recommends that lay people participate in this worldwide worship. There is no reason why children on occasion and for short periods of time cannot be slowly introduced to this practice. At first they may just listen while Mom and Dad pray part of the office. Later they may be invited to say the Our Father and the Glory Be with their parents. A few words, very few, of explanation at the beginning of an hour can introduce the youngsters to what is about to happen.

Family quiet times and places

Healthy silence is not a mere negation. Rather it is a favored opportunity for conversation—it just depends on with whom one wants to speak. People who care much about each other desire occasional times and places to be alone for their conversations. Dating is an obvious example. Phone booths are another. Husbands and wives in a happy marriage seek these times together when they are feasible. This natural human need for communing si-

lences was raised to the supernatural level by Jesus himself
in his habitual and long periods of solitude prayerfully immersed in the Father. He likewise taught that in ordinary
homes the faithful are to go "to their private rooms, close
the door and pray to the Father in secret" (Mt 6:6). The
most privileged place for prayer is, of course, in the presence of the Blessed Sacrament, even though this blessing
is not always possible (see CCC 2691).

In fostering prayer and quiet, parents should not, of
course, be overbearing or nagging toward one another or
the children. Yet at the same time the Gospel is written
for everyone, as we have just noted in Matthew 6:6. Just
as Mom and Dad expect quiet when a family member
is ill or is catching up on missed sleep, so they can also
teach by example and word that there are quiet times for
prayer. Children then understand better how and why we
consider a happy home to be "the domestic sanctuary of
the Church".

13

Prayer in a Busy Life

One of the more formidable challenges the beginner in prayer must face is that of the pressures of work and other duties: "How do I fit everything into twenty-four hours?" Especially in our contemporary world many people have so many commitments that they feel simply unable to give communing with God the time it requires. Prayer becomes something added on to all the other concerns of life—if and when, they conclude, it can be cared for at all.

Hence we begin by asking a down-to-earth question: Is "ample time for prayer" a realistic ideal in modern life? We must honestly face the fact that many of us are time pressured, burdened under work overloads, "stressed out". Medical studies and surveys claim that too many of our contemporaries get insufficient sleep. Health suffers, and sometimes so do human relationships.

I shall not in this chapter presume to offer anyone a detailed blueprint for how to organize one's life hour by hour. This I do not know for others. In any event details are for each adult to decide, with principles derived from divine revelation and by the lead of the Holy Spirit—and with the aid of sound spiritual direction, if such is available. (See SSD, pp. 165–67, 195–96.) However, we can suggest some basic guidelines for thinking rightly about this problem.

Sound perspectives

First of all, when our life is properly ordered, there is not the least clash between prayer, on the one hand, and work or other relationships, on the other. There are difficulties to be solved, of course. But if we have our priorities in order, if we make sound choices, our human and divine duties fit smoothly together. Actually each of them contributes to the welfare of the others. To grasp how this happens we need only read the lives of the saints: married, religious, and clerical. The saints have the knack for getting things right.

Secondly, we should recall that time given to meditative and contemplative prayer is time given to those dearest to us: wife, husband, children, parishioners, students, those we serve. Far-sighted people easily see this. The best thing each of us can do for those we love is to become a saint, a man or woman of deep prayer. Our influence for their good is then powerful and eternal. Mediocre husbands and wives provide food, clothing, and shelter in their homes, and these goods are important, but they may contribute little to the eternal good of their families and those they serve. The same is true of lukewarm priests and religious. Sometimes the mediocre do harm in what matters most.

Thirdly, we all know that exceptionally pressured days and situations can and do occur. Emergencies, small and great, do pop up; exceptions do happen. Sometimes we just cannot have the time for prayer that we have planned. Yet an occasional impossibility does not harm prayer life —we are loving God in another way. We are speaking here of the usual, the normal well-ordered life. As long as exceptions remain exceptions and do not become the rule, we have no serious problem.

Fourthly, we should try to avoid being overly anxious and unduly stressed with time pressures. Yet we should also avoid wasting time, for example, with idle gossiping or useless and often harmful television. Usually we should get sufficient sleep and rest. We do well to recall Jesus' admonition to the weary apostles: "You *must* go away and rest for a while." We should notice, too, that this precept is found in a time-pressured situation (Mk 6:30–32).

Lastly, Jesus himself is our first model here as well as in all things. Though his contemporaries needed his ministrations endlessly more than people need your attention and mine, yet he habitually went off for long and frequent times of solitude and deep prayer with the Father. See again Mark 1:35 and Luke 5:16. What he did himself, he tells us to do, all of us: "When you pray, go into your room, close the door and pray to your Father in secret" (Mt 6:6). We will come out of that room far better for others than when we entered it.

The divine realism

There is no doubt that human relationships, just like working and recreating, have an irreplaceable importance in anyone's life. Yet the divine vision of a fruitful and fulfilled life is far more focused, comprehensive, and real than ours. The simple fact is that you and I, whatever our age may be, are not long for this world. We are soon to die. A baby being born as you read this sentence is not here for long either: seventy, eighty, or even ninety years is a mere flick next to eternity. In this life all of us are pilgrims on the way to one of two alternatives: eternal ecstasy or eternal disaster. There are no other choices. Work and recreation, activity and rest, programs and politics are means to our final goal. They are not goals in themselves.

Sacred Scripture could not be more clear about what comes first and what comes second and third on this road to our destiny. Our ultimate aim is never said to be work. Rather it is no less than an enthralling communing with the Lord of glory. Psalm 11:7 lays it down that God loves authenticity, goodness, and virtue so much that their reward is no less than unending delight: a love-filled immersion in purest Beauty for all eternity. Psalm 16:11 has the same message: We are called to experience unending joy in the divine presence, not merely some limited and humanly contrived substitute. We have seen and heard nothing that begins to compare with it. We cannot even imagine what the Lord has in store for those who love him. It is inexpressible (1 Cor 2:9; 1 Pet 1:8).

To make sense here below of the intensely busy lives

that most of us live there is no other way than to get
our basic principles straight. God's word has it that both
here and hereafter communing with him, gazing on his
beauty, is our overriding necessity, the most important
thing we have to do. Prayer is not, therefore, something
added on to all the rest, merely squeezed in here or there.
Rather only in God do we find our basic reason for being,
our fulfillment as persons (Ps 62:1, 5). We are to make
him our supreme joy, and thus find the only complete
answer to our hearts' desires (Ps 37:4). This analysis is,
of course, the exact opposite of what the worldly person
thinks. But a consistent theist cannot hold otherwise. Are
you consistent? Am I?

Integrating prayer and work: Gospel guides

To help us see things as they really are in the multiplic-
ities of daily life (no easy task), we need to keep before
our mind's eye some basic principles. We will mention
a few of them.

1. Work is not prayer. It sometimes happens that a
confessor or a retreat master, when questioned about the
time pressure problem and the curtailment of prayer, will
give the pat answer, "Well, just make your work a prayer,
and all will be fine." Simplistic answers are either mis-
leading or false. This one is both. Scripture flatly denies
that work is prayer. They are very different (Sir 38:27—
39:6), even though we offer both to God's glory (1 Cor
10:31). Jesus in his own life distinguishes his long and
habitual times in solitary prayer from his works of teaching, healing, and forming the apostles. The latter do not

interfere with the former. The apostles in turn make the same distinction in their lives and find no conflict (Acts 6:4). Vatican Council II has the same message for all the faithful. Every one of us is to be "eager to act and devoted to contemplation". Moreover, the first is to be subordinated to the second (SC, no. 2).

2. Enthusiasm deepens as prayer deepens. Our English word, "enthusiasm", comes from the Greek, *en theos*, that is, possessed by God. As most people advance in age they tend to lose something of their natural liveliness, but something deeper should be taking over: growth in love for God. They who love much, live much. We should be more enthusiastic at sixty than we were at sixteen. The saints are that way. The love given by the Holy Spirit is an energy that overcomes our inertia, laziness, drifting, apathy, dullness. The person who loves much, does much. Time for prayer, therefore, is time given to other people.

3. The most fruitful activity flows from contemplative depth. Love in the heart of the Church, mainly in her saints, is the mainspring that drives her evangelizing (2 Cor 5:14). The enthusiasm of which we speak is born and grows in contemplative solitude and liturgical worship. This is why we read that "happy is the man who ponders the law of the Lord day and night. . . . He is like a tree planted next to the streams of a river. . . . Success attends all he does" (Ps 1:1–3). This is why, too, Pope John XXIII said of cloistered nuns that they hold the first place in the apostolate of the Church through their love, prayer, and sacrifice.

4. Perseverance in commitment and suffering is rooted in a burning love for the indwelling Trinity. Men and

women of prayer are faithful to their Lord who is the truth, and so they fearlessly proclaim his undiluted message in their lives and in their words. Their motivation is pure and their manner is daring (2 Cor 4:1–2; Phil 1:14–15). Like the prophet Jeremiah, they accept unpopularity: "The word of the Lord has brought me insult and derision through the day" (Jer 20:8). All of this demands personal depth; it is no mere human inclination. Prayer promotes the best of action. There is no least clash between them.

5. Finally, deep communion with God produces happy and attractive apostles, men and women radiant with joy (Ps 34:5; 1 Pet 1:8) and warm in their love of others (Acts 20:36–38; 2 Cor 2:4; Phil 4:1). They are walking advertisements for the beauty of the message they proclaim in words.

It is no wonder, therefore, that Pope John Paul II has so emphasized a deep immersion in the Trinity, both in his life and in his words. For us lesser ones as well this immersion is our first duty, a duty that promotes the best accomplishment of all other duties.

The oasis of silence

Few of our contemporaries need to be persuaded that much of our modern world is beset with incessant noise: traffic clatter, radio and television, lawn mowers and jet planes, household appliances and human chatter. Thoughtful men and women, even those reflecting a secular point of view, are well aware of the detrimental effects a continuing din has on our psyches. In his best seller, *Future*

Shock, Alvin Toffler wrote about "the overstimulated individual . . . the bombardment of the senses . . . information overload . . . decision stress". Thomas Merton observed that "We live in a society whose whole policy is to excite every nerve in the human body and keep it at the highest pitch of artificial tension, to strain every human desire to the limit and to create as many new desires and synthetic passions as possible, in order to cater to them with the products of our factories and printing presses and movie studios and all the rest." This, he explained, is why he had chosen to "live in the woods".

We are not speaking of an anti-social isolation. Nor do we envision here a rejection of normal human contacts and healthy recreation. The Lord and his saints most generously gave of themselves to others.

Yet the fact remains that our psychic energies are limited, just as our physical ones are. We need mental and emotional rest, rest from overstimulation, if we are to be normal and healthy. All the more do we need a respite from clatter if we are to be prayerful. Such are intervals of healthy solitude and silence.

There remains another angle to all this. Paradoxically, a serious conversation requires seclusion and quiet. This is often why one person may invite another to dinner, and why we have silent library reading rooms. This is why Jesus himself habitually went off to be alone with the Father. The Master is our primary model.

On learning to be quiet

We seldom, if ever, seek negations for the sake of negations. Our reason is something positive. We fast on occasion, not because food is bad, but because we want to become total in our love and be rid of all impediments to it. In self-denial we empty ourselves to become full and complete. So also with silence: we are seeking all the goods described in this chapter.

One of the most widespread problems in modern technological societies is learning how to *be*, yes, simply to be: to be alive and free of a hundred differing pressures that impede a healthy, peaceful awareness of ourselves and of our immediate environment. Strange as it may sound, we need to learn to become quiet, to enjoy being alive to reality. Most of all we need to become sensitive to the divine omnipresence. As the psalmist put it, "Be quiet and know that I am God" (Ps 46:10).

A relaxed awareness does not happen automatically. Learning this openness to reality requires some explicit attention and effort. We need occasionally to get away from the crowd, to find or make a place of solitude. Then we may gaze slowly at a sunset or a tree, a banana or a carrot or a leaf. We consider its colors, shapes, textures, and tiny details proclaiming tiny beauties. Slowly we imbibe each thing's splendors. We enjoy it quietly. We are be-ing. We are on the way to learning to be quiet. We are also better prepared for prayer, ready to receive the gentle loving awareness or yearning for God that he gives to uncluttered people.

Solitude: What and why

What precisely is this be-ing, this quiet awareness, this openness for everything? First of all, as we have just noted, solitude is not isolation, a dislike for and avoidance of people. Most of us are not called to be hermits, and even hermits are to be in touch with others especially through their prayer. Isolation is unhealthy.

Biblical solitude is outgoing—first of all to one's supreme Beloved, and then to all others in him. Anyone in love needs and wants to be alone with the dear one, at least on occasion. These favored times are alive with expansive love that eventually touches many other people as well. When God in the Old Testament seeks to win his bride, his people, back to himself, he lures her into the wilderness and there speaks to her heart (Hos 2:14). This sacred aloneness is one of the many reasons we make retreats: to be touched by the divine fire.

What are some other reasons? As we have already remarked, we need psychic rest from the tumult and frenetic activities of contemporary life. To avoid suffocation we need to be immersed in the supreme One. Without the calming effects of periods of quiet we cannot live the continual prayer themes of Scripture: keeping the eyes of our minds always on the Lord (Ps 25:15), singing to him in our hearts when our minds are free, avoiding useless gossip that profits no one and only too often harms (Mt 12:36).

In our prayer lives we are also to relive Jesus' great periods of solitude, even if not to the same radical degree. Long before dawn he would go off to pray in the wilderness or on the mountain. After relating to and teaching the crowds he would again go off to the hills to commune with the Father. On another occasion he prayed all night before choosing the twelve apostles. All this, we are told, he did over and over again. It was his habit (Mk 1:35; 6:46; Lk 5:16; 6:12; 9:18, 28; 21:37).

While it is no surprise that saintly priests and bishops, monks and nuns all follow faithfully this example of their Lord, many people would probably not expect that married saints do likewise. But they do, and none of them neglects other people. They follow what Jesus told them and us to do: Have a place in our home where we can be alone with the Father, Son, and Holy Spirit, and there commune with the blessed Trinity. This is a radical condition for the "one thing" readily to happen: gazing on the beauty of the Lord.

PART FOUR

QUESTIONS AND PROBLEMS

14

When Should We Pray?

You may wonder at the title of this chapter, not because of the question itself (which makes sense to any serious theist) but because a whole chapter is devoted to its answer. Most people assume that it is quite enough to pray in the morning upon rising, even if only for two or three minutes (and usually much less), in the evening, and before and after meals.

In our previous chapter we considered perspectives and principles that may serve as sound guides to integrating set times for prayer into the hectic schedules many of us face on a daily basis. We now wish to extend our thoughts into the context of our unspeakable triune God and the lofty biblical ideal of a communion worthy of his splendor. We wish to look more closely into the biblical theme of continual prayer. Libraries have been produced about Jesus, his person, and his message—and new insights continue to abound. No end is in sight. Nor is it a surprise that the beloved disciple, who leaned on the Lord's breast at the last supper, brings his Gospel to a close with the remark that if everything about the Lord

were recorded, the world probably could not hold all the
books that would have to be written (Jn 21:25). When,
then, we ask, should we converse with and be immersed
in triune Beauty, Father, Son, and Holy Spirit? Be ready
for surprises; the universe is full of them.

Favored times for prayer

The inspired word of Scripture gives two answers to the
question we raise in this chapter. There are special occa-
sions for communing with the indwelling Trinity. And
then there is a praying to him on a continuing basis (Eph
5:19–20). Both answers are insisted upon, and yet there
is no conflict, no incompatibility between them. Anyone
who has been head over heels in genuine love has at least
a beginning glimpse into what this latter may mean: to
commune with God always and everywhere.

But we consider first the favored times, and we take our
lead from the Church's official prayer, the Liturgy of the
Hours. (We assume that the Mass is the pinnacle of each
day.) Seven other times each day the Church turns to her
Lord: early morning, midmorning, noon, midafternoon,
evening, before bedtime—and then there is the "hour of
readings", which can be inserted in an interval best suited
to each person's or community's situation or preference.
This last is not a sixty-minute hour; it takes about twenty
minutes when it is recited, longer when it is sung. See
chapter 11 above for details.

In addition to the Liturgy of the Hours the special
times would include one's ordinary vocal prayers on rising and retiring, grace before and after meals, the rosary,

the way of the cross. Likewise the periods we reserve for meditation or contemplation are especially favored. As we have already pointed out, contemplation is so special that Scripture calls it the "one thing", the most important thing anyone has to do.

As we have earlier said in chapter 9, contemplation occurs in two forms: delightful and dry. Both are profitable, the first to encourage us and to draw us to fidelity, the second to purify and strengthen us. It may be difficult for people to appreciate that arid waiting prayer can be "favored", but it is. Lovers wait. They are used to it. To win Rachel, Jacob worked and waited seven years, and they seemed to him "like a few days so much did he love her" (Gen 29:20). Over and over does the biblical word speak of our "waiting patiently for the Lord" (Ps 37:7; 40:1; 105:4; 119:81–82, 123; see also FW, pp. 68, 165, 171–73, 221–23; SSD, pp. 160, 185, 200–201).

While our periods for mental prayer can be placed at any time of the day or night according to our circumstances, there is no doubt that Jesus and his saints had a predilection for vigil prayer during the night and dawn prayer, even "long before dawn" (Mk 1:35; Lk 6:12; 5:16). This preference continues on in our own day. Prayerful men and women commonly say that they favor communing with the Lord early in the morning and/or at a time during the night. It is not difficult to understand why: these are the quiet times for most of us, and at dawn we are refreshed and much less distracted.

Continual prayer

We now consider what some people think is fantastic, unreal. If you are time-pressured, you may assume it is impossible. So perhaps we should begin with a few reflections about the idea and reality of awesome things. Our universe is full of them. They are hard to believe, and they range all the way from the atomic world to the billions of galaxies, quasars, and supernovas (see EPB, chapters 7, 8, 9). You yourself are amazing. Your enzyme system alone is almost incredible. As you read this paragraph about three billion cells in your body have died, and another three billion have been born.

We do well to get used to wondrous realities—continual prayer is one of them. As we get closer and closer to infinite Wonder, we better and better grasp what all this implies. After all, the consummate Artist is the purest, endless, unfathomable amazement.

"My eyes [that is, the attention of my mind] are always on the Lord" (Ps 25:15). Yes, that idea is fantastic, hard to take both literally and seriously. But there is more to it, much more than we can deal with in this primer. A taste will have to suffice. After a sampling we shall then explain what the taste refers to.

Already in the Old Testament saintly men and women were praising and blessing the Lord continually (Ps 145:1–2, 21), meditating on his word day and night (Ps 1:1–2; Josh 1:8), seeking his presence untiringly (1 Chron 16:11). As people genuinely in love like to do, they linger in the divine presence, remembering the Beloved and keeping their attention on him through the night (Ps 16:8;

63:6). Even when God seems far away and their prayer dry, they are content to wait for him patiently; they continue in waiting for his consolation and saving help (Ps 119:123; 40:1; 37:7).

Following the example of Jesus, New Testament writers are of the same mind. They engage in continuous prayer, singing to the Lord in their hearts always and everywhere, never losing heart, retaining a constant happiness and an indescribable peace (Lk 5:16; Eph 5:19–20; Col 3:16–17; Lk 18:1; 1 Thess 5:17; Phil 4:4, 6–7; see also FW, pp. 191–92, 213–14; and CCC 2697–99; 2742–43).

Interpretation and practice

How do we understand this extraordinary love affair with purest Beauty, who is God? We should not fail to emphasize the obvious: he is, after all, endless loveliness. Great things are bound to happen to people who take him seriously. When that sinks in sufficiently, we then recall that every human person is, as a spirit-in-the-flesh being, thirsty for unending goodness, truth, and beauty. Created things, being finite, never completely fill us. Always we want more. And sin never satisfies. It cannot. As the psalmist expressed it, "Only in God is my soul at rest", the refreshing rest of one who is being entirely filled (Ps 62:1). Therefore, a deepening and continuing immersion in him makes complete sense. It is and must be the "one thing".

Further, we cannot attain to constant prayer by ourselves, no matter how hard we try to be free of distractions. In a gradual process of growth, both in our depth of prayer and in living the gospel generously, it is God himself who brings about the transformation. One of the traits of the summit, the transforming union, is that the soul is so strongly united with the indwelling Trinity that it continually perceives a deep-down, delightful presence of the Father, the Son, and their Holy Spirit. This experience does not interfere with work or with one's attention to or concern for others. (See FW, pp. 105–6.)

Finally, on the way to the summit there are times of lingering prayer. Just as people who love much are used to waiting, so also do they enjoy lingering with the beloved one: just being present to each other with or without words and in differing degrees of intensity. "I keep the Lord before me always . . . all night long . . . living through love in his presence" (Ps 16:8; 63:6; Col 3:1–2). Such is the way saints live, and they are our models. The prayerful person is never dull and dreary. Boredom is banished.

15

Problems and Pitfalls

Being present to and conversing with one we love is the most normal, simple, and easy thing in the world. And of all who know and love us, our indwelling Creator— more intimate to us than we are to ourselves—clearly is number one. Yet because we are wounded and live in a world of almost endless complexities, we have not a few difficulties in communing with him. In the course of this primer we have in various ways touched upon a number of these challenges and puzzles. Yet it may be helpful in this chapter to proceed by way of some additional questions you yourself may have, things we have not yet dealt with.

1. *"I often think I am too busy to pray as I would like to, and yet I wonder if I am rationalizing with reasons that may sound valid but really are not."*

Unless you are close to being a saint, and if you do not give prominence to prayer in your life, it is likely that there is at least some rationalizing going on. Let me suggest to you a checklist that may help you decide. Just ask yourself the following questions and ponder each one of them quietly before the Lord. Is God really number one with me? Is this priority in words only, or also in my everyday decisions? Why really do I watch this television program or engage in that conversation? Do I often reflect that I am only a pilgrim here on earth, here only for a short while—and do I think of my eternity as I ought? Am I convinced that the closer I am to the Lord in prayer, the better I will be for everyone else? Does this conviction much affect what I do—and what I fail to do? Is my busyness often due to much ado about nothing? Do I use my time wisely? Would I accept my husband (wife, close friend) saying to me "I have no time to spend with you"? Have I weighed carefully how saints in my state of life handle this rationalizing problem?

2. *"Sometimes I don't feel like praying, and sometimes I do. It seems that this is not a sound guide to follow in practice. Am I right?"*

Yes, you are. The world would be chaotic if all of us did only what we were inclined to do. No place of business, no hospital, school, government, police force, no mother or father can responsibly operate chiefly according to feelings. We are to live with the guidance of reason enlightened by the divine word. Further, the Lord judges us, not according to our emotions and sentiments (which to a large extent we cannot control), but according to our free decisions (which we can control). Then, too, we recall that unfeeling prayer can be most beneficial, indeed precious.

3. *"I am often pestered with distractions at prayer. I really do not want them, but is there anything I can do to get rid of them? I try but don't much succeed."*

The first thing you can do is to be at peace. As long as distractions are not deliberate and intentional, they do much less harm than you may think. If you sincerely want to pray, and you try reasonably well, you are praying. As St. Teresa put it, "Your will is with his Majesty." Gently turn your mind back to him when you notice that it has strayed. You are succeeding. (See FW, pp. 223–26; SSD, p. 198; CCC 2729.)

4. *"I have a weak self-image. I do not think I am worth much. How can I imagine that God loves me intimately when I don't love myself? How can I feel close to him?"*

This is a problem, of course, but it is not hopeless. Speaking with someone who understands self-image problems can be a help. Full healing may take time, but if you try peacefully to believe people who do express concern and love for you, healing can be furthered. And if with some guidance you understand how your weak self-image came about (usually it happened early in life, when you were a child), you can begin to see that indeed you are very valuable. Most of all remember that Jesus was tortured to death, so much did he love you. And he loves you still, personally and individually. And so does Mary, our most loving Mother and the Queen of heaven. No one has ever turned to her in his need and been left unaided. You may also read the advice given in SSD, pp. 194–95.

5. *"I'm afraid my prayer isn't worth much—and I am not now referring to a self-image problem. When I read or hear about the saints and their burning contemplation, I get discouraged. My progress is so slow. I am a sinner, and I have been a big sinner. How could I ever hope to reach their heights?"*

There are several answers to this difficulty. First of all, some of the saints also began as big sinners: Mary Magdalen and Augustine, for example. If you are as determined to change as they were, you also can reach sublime love and holiness. In one of his homilies St. Bernard was speaking about the universal call to the summit of contemplation. He then addressed your very question by saying that no matter into what depths of slime (that was his word!) a sinner has fallen, he is still called to the heights. After all, God's mercy *is* infinite. Secondly, your prayer can become most valuable. For you also it can be the "one thing", more precious than your work and fun times. Thirdly, even if you are now on the lowest rung of sanctity, but are faithful to the light and love given you there, God will raise you to the next rung, and then the next, and the next. Fourthly, we should not forget the great rejoicing in heaven over even one sinner who repents. No less than twice does Jesus emphasize this point (Lk 15:7, 10). Lastly, do not judge your prayer's value by the degree of your feelings. Recall St. Teresa's comment that the best prayer is the prayer that produces the virtues.

Remember also that the worst reaction to discouragement is to give up praying.

6. *"What should I do when I really want to meditate or to be with God in a simple awareness of him, but nothing comes? I feel blah and empty; nothing happens. It gets very discouraging, and I feel as though I am wasting time. I could be doing something else worthwhile. I get close to giving up the whole thing."*

Of all the questions I am asked about prayer this one is either at the top of the list or close to it. You have expressed it well, and you have lots of company. Unless instructed well, almost everyone assumes without question that this empty feeling is clear proof that he is getting nowhere in his prayer life. A number of things need to be noted. First of all, if this "blah" situation is due to willed mediocrity, cutting corners with God, knowingly not giving him everything, then indeed it is bad. The emptiness is real, and the solution is simple: Repent! (See Rev 3:1–3.) Begin to be fully generous in your state in life, and give the Lord everything he asks of you—and remember that what he asks is always for your own good.

However, if you are sincerely trying to be generous, be at peace. This empty feeling is then actually beneficial, because it is purifying you of defects. An unfeeling, dry desire for God is not only good; it is necessary. Reaching out to him without any felt satisfaction purifies a person of defects that impede greater intimacy. I can assure you from long experience that this is perhaps the hardest lesson for beginners to learn: an empty-feeling desire for God is precious prayer. This hard-to-believe truth is

related to how and why the Father gives his wisdom to
the little, humble ones, as Jesus himself so beautifully
said (Lk 10:21). Most people assume that it is Scripture
scholars and theologians who through years of study understand God best. But actually it is the little ones and
those who love most that have the deepest insights born
of intimacy: "All those who love are begotten by God and
know him" (1 Jn 4:7). Hence, unless scholars are saintly,
their knowledge is more verbal than deep. (See FW, pp.
220–23; SSD, pp. 159–60.)

Once again the saints are examples of our point. St.
Thérèse of Lisieux's love was burning and heroic, and
yet she often did not feel it emotionally. It was in her
will. And her love became all the deeper because of the
darkness. Jesus himself put the matter perfectly: "From
their fruits you shall know them" (Mt 7:20). St. John of
the Cross spells out the Lord's teaching in his doctrine
of the purifying benefits of the two nights of sense and
spirit. They are times when nothing is felt and God seems
far away: no cozy sensations, no delight, no consolation.
In the second night the person even feels abandoned by
God, though he remains most dear to the Lord. All is
well. Fear not. (See Ps 63:1; FW, chapter 9, "Fire in the
Nights", pp. 159–74; CCC 2731.)

7. *"What should we think of new prayer movements and ideas
such as New Age, Buddhist and other oriental techniques, and
centering prayer?"*

New Age writings are so intellectually empty of sub-
stance, they are not worth writing about. The best thing

to do is simply bypass them. To take them seriously is to be led astray.

8. *"You seem to imply that Buddhist contemplation and centering prayer are worth discussing. If that is so, suppose we begin with a few words about Buddhist prayer."*

The first thing to note is that Buddhist awareness is neither contemplation nor prayer. They say so themselves. Yet there are sincere people who wonder whether all types of contemplation, whether occidental or oriental, are not after all pretty much the same. While God can touch any person with his grace, and even though the Hindu and the Buddhist can readily realize more or less clearly that this visible world cannot be all that there is, yet the leaders of the latter insist that Buddhism is not a religion. While it entails a world view and a moral path, its teaching is not concerned with the supreme God, the Lord who is to be loved and worshipped. We are theists, while Buddhist leaders teach agnosticism. That is, they neither deny nor affirm God. We have two fundamentally different outlooks on reality; we live in two very diverse universes.

Hence, it follows secondly that a Buddhist awareness produced by human techniques and methods is radically different from our theistic contemplation. Our communion with the living God is completely interpersonal, intensely so: we adore, love, praise, thirst for our triune Beloved. This we have seen throughout these pages. What the Buddhist describes is entirely impersonal, not at all a relationship between persons, let alone an intimate one. We can hope that the individual Buddhist of good will responds to the grace of the living God, but he does not hear about this real God from his cultural milieu. For the Buddhist, as Thomas Merton put it, "reality becomes aware of itself in me."

Thirdly, as we have already noted, our infused contemplation can in no way be produced by methods and techniques. It is the Lord who feeds the hungry with good things (Lk 1:53), he and no other. As St. Teresa of Avila observed, we cannot by our efforts produce the least spark of contemplative prayer. For the Buddhist the attainment of his enlightenment is entirely the result of human efforts.

Fourthly, for us the divinely given love communion grows not only in depth but also in duration up to the point where it becomes continual in the transforming union. For the Buddhist, *satori* enlightenment is brief. As one of their leaders (Suzuki) put it, if the awareness is long, it is not *satori*.

Fifthly, in my study of Buddhism I do not recall even once reading the word "love" used in connection with their inner awareness. On the other hand, our contemplation is a love matter before all else, a loving with our whole heart, mind, and strength, a love poured out by the Holy Spirit himself (Rom 5:5).

Lastly, the final aim of the Buddhist enterprise is the cessation of desires and suffering, a negative result or outcome, surely a dreary prospect at best. Our Christ-centered destiny, on the other hand, is to be "filled with the utter fullness of God himself", and thus to be crowned with a delight that cannot be put into words (Eph 3:19;

1 Pet 1:8). Eye has not seen, nor ear heard, indeed, we cannot imagine what God has prepared for those who love him (1 Cor 2:9).

9. *"What do you think of centering prayer? It has been both widely promoted and also attacked. Do you think it is helpful?"*

The simple answer to your question is No, I do not. Rather it is more of a hindrance to contemplative prayer. It seems that the promoters of centering prayer have recently been changing their message, due perhaps to criticism. However, I shall respond to what has been generally presented to many people. Centering methods have been much influenced by oriental ideas, and that is the main problem. For the sake of clarity and brevity, I shall make three points. The first is that one should beware of techniques for emptying the mind to prepare it for contemplation. This is unnatural. Our minds are made to be filled, not emptied. Nowhere does Scripture advise this. Rather the beginner is told to fill his mind by pondering the word of God day and night (Ps 1:1-2). This is meditation, not emptying our minds. St. Teresa rightly said that when we are ready, God gives us something better than our efforts can produce, namely infused communing with himself. This we have explained in chapters 8 and 9.

Secondly, it is an illusion to think that techniques can produce an immersion in God. He is not one to be manipulated as one can manipulate a machine or appliance. And thirdly, emptying methods can frustrate both the beginner who needs input on which to reflect and the advanced person who needs freedom from human efforts to be able to receive the light and love God wishes to communicate. (See also FW, pp. 51, 92; SSD, pp. 171–72, 184, 202–4.)

16

Quick Questions

In this chapter we will follow the question/answer procedure that hopefully served our previous chapter, that is, asking questions and then responding to them as briefly as possible.

1. *"Is it helpful for beginners in prayer to belong to the charismatic renewal? What are your thoughts about this movement?"*

Much good has come both to individuals and to the Church through the zeal and devotion of men and women in the charismatic renewal. It is true that occasional aberrations can occur among members of any devotional group, but to keep these to a minimum I would suggest several helps to proper discernment and practice: (a) A sound enterprise welcomes the guidance of the Church —this provides wholeness and balance in embracing all of the Church's immensely rich and beautiful prayer traditions: private and vocal prayer, meditation, contemplation, Liturgy of the Hours, Mass. (b) What we have said in chapter 7 about excessive vocal prayers should be kept

in mind. (c) Like all the rest of us, members of the charismatic renewal also need "an abundance of contemplation"
(LG, no. 41), and they should provide amply for it in their
lives. (See also SSD, pp. 162–63, 172–76.)

2. *"We have already considered the biblical ideal, so well lived
by the saints, of praying continually. Here on earth, of course,
this is most fully lived in the transforming union, but it seems
to me that life is full of invitations to raise our minds and hearts
to God. This is true, is it not?"*

Yes, it is most true. We can speak of triggers leading us to
pray through the day. For mental prayer we can call them
atmosphere setters or springboards. For a man or woman
attuned to the divine, almost anything can occasion the
thought of God: a leaf closely observed . . . another person's smile or scowl . . . a tree . . . a bird's song . . . a
Gospel scene . . . a disappointment, a failure, or a success . . . a headline . . . an illness . . . a police siren . . .
passing a church and a tabernacle . . . growing old . . .
a crucifix . . . a downpour or a blizzard . . . a nameless
yearning that has no limits. The possibilities are endless.
(See SSD, pp. 192–93.)

3. *"It seems to me that in order to meditate we need either a
vivid imagination or a supply of lofty thoughts, and yet I have
very few, if any. All I seem able to do is to repeat words or
someone else's ideas and petitions."*

While it is true that people differ a great deal in their
imaginative capacities, yet it is likely that you are un-

derestimating yourself. Success in meditation is not due
first of all to a lively imagination but to much love. So
also with lofty ideas. Scripture takes it for granted that
very simple people can ponder the divine word "day and
night". They too can carry out Jesus' admonition to go
to their private room, close the door, and commune with
the Father in secret. And the Lord added immediately that
not only we need not, but we should not babble many
words at prayer (Mt 6:6–7). Rather we are to emphasize
pondering his person and his word.

4. *"But I have heard and read about people who can meditate
for an hour or two. The best I can do is to pray for a few minutes,
and then my mind strays off. Is this problem common?"*

Yes, it is very common. The first thing to do about it is to
recall what we said in our last chapter about distractions.
It is a hard lesson to learn, one that requires repetition.
Then, too, remember that babies begin to speak by utter-
ing a word or two. They do not worry about expressing
themselves in long sentences or giving speeches. Living
things grow slowly, and so does our power to carry on
a conversation with others and with God. We need patience, perseverance, and mostly love.

5. *"Yet the saints, and sometimes other people as well, seem so
absorbed in God . . ."*

Yes, they often are, but usually they too have begun at
the beginning like you and me. As we have already noted,
if you remain faithful in living the gospel generously in

your state in life, and if you are committed to your times for meditation and contemplation, you too will grow in "living through love" in the divine presence (Eph 1:4).

6. *"What should I do when I get fidgety or restless at prayer?"*

This problem is akin to the distraction question, and so what we said on that topic can be useful here. Further, an adequate amount of sleep should contribute to solving the fatigue problem and the restlessness related to it. Sleep experts agree that many Americans are notably sleep deprived, and this is probably true as well in other contemporary technological and wealthy societies. Third, you might change your praying position from kneeling to sitting or standing or vice versa—or, if possible, get up and walk back and forth in a quiet place. St. Teresa herself advised this latter when one is antsy. Fourth, be patient and remember that fidelity in this difficulty itself can further prayer growth. And last of all, never give up your meditation or contemplation. Most likely things will eventually brighten up. (See FW, p. 223; SSD, pp. 180–81.)

7. *"When we grow into the beginnings of infused contemplation and the following stages, is it important to know where we are in these developments? Some people say that knowing this is not important."*

They are mistaken, very much so. Unless you have a competent spiritual director who does know where you are and is guiding you accordingly, you definitely should know. St. Teresa gives about a half dozen reasons why this is so. One could add several more. (See FW, pp. 73–76.) Let me mention one basic reason. What we ought to do in our mental prayer and how we are to operate varies a great deal according to our stage of development. To attempt to read and meditate when God is giving contemplative light and love impedes the blessing. Unwittingly the person is rejecting a marvelous gift of growth. Another example: unless one is guided rightly or recognizes that he is in one of the two dark nights and knows what to do in it, his progress is going to be hindered. Our next question offers a third example.

8. *"Sometimes when I am doing spiritual reading, or during Mass or meditation, all of a sudden I feel very close to God. It is delightful and I seem to be absorbed in him for several minutes. There are no distractions. What should I do? I don't want to resist what he seems to be giving. Am I imagining something? I don't want to be under an illusion."*

If you are living the gospel generously in your daily life, most likely this is a deeper experience of infused contemplative prayer. When it occurs during meditation or spiritual reading, just gladly accept what the Lord is giving and leave aside for that time your thinking or reading. Follow his lead: you are giving up the lesser for the greater. When this occurs during Mass, it is good to try gently to attend to what is going on during the liturgy. But if you cannot pay attention because the experience is so deep, there is no need to worry. The Lord is in charge, and he knows what is best for you. (You might reread chapter 9 on contemplation and see FW, pp. 68–69, 94.)

9. *"Is it a good idea to have a spiritual director as a guide for growing in prayer?"*

Yes, if you can find one who is competent, prayerful, sound of judgment, and faithful to the mind of the Church. But if he lacks these qualities, it is better to look for someone else who does have them. A knowledgeable guide can be of great help in applying principles to you and to your situation—for example, in aiding you with questions 7 and 8 above, and much else. (See FW, pp. 297–98; SSD, pp. 64–69, 75–79, 104.)

10. *"How can I find this kind of director? They seem to be scarce."*

I am afraid I must agree with you. I hear of this problem repeatedly. People tell me over and over that they cannot find a competent guide who can help them get closer to God in prayer. St. Teresa made this same comment in the sixteenth century. What you might do is to look for a priest who is himself prayerful, who gives enlightened homilies, and who is of the mind of the Church. However, this question cannot be answered completely in a few sentences. Hence, the best advice is to read SSD, pp. 102–6, and FW, pp. 289–94, 299–303.

11. *"Do you think that keeping a prayer journal is a good idea, that is, writing down my experiences at prayer, and later on reviewing what I have said in the journal?"*

A prayer journal is a means to an end, not something one does for its own sake. Thus we should judge it on the basis of whether it does us good or not. Surely vanity about "what I have done or achieved" is not a good reason. If journaling brings about genuine benefit, and if one does not spend too much time with it, it may be useful. But if little or nothing solid results, it would be better to spend the time in further prayer.

12. *"Is it enough to pray individually by oneself, or should we also join with others in our family, parish, convent, school, nursing home?"*

Yes, we should participate in community prayer, and most of all at Mass and the Liturgy of the Hours. Private devotions such as the family rosary are beneficial, but we should not so multiply them that we have little time for meditation and contemplation. Once again we need to remember that Scripture terms contemplation the "one thing", the overriding necessity in human life. Yet there are several reasons why we should also engage in community prayer. One is that Jesus is especially present when we gather in his name (Mt 18:19-20; see also SSD, pp. 175-76). A second reason is that we are social beings, and thus we should give communal witness to God and to his primary place in our lives. A third is that in our group prayers we support one another and give good example. We are building up the Mystical Body of Christ as well as our individual spiritual lives.

17

Assessing Progress

Beginners in prayer invariably assume as obvious (and often it takes years to get over the assumption) that they are growing in their prayer lives only when they enjoy pleasant feelings, consolations, and delight in their devotions. They sometimes think that they are listening to the Holy Spirit when actually they may be welcoming their own preferences and persuasions. On the other hand, it is equally obvious to them, if not more so, that their prayer is nothing, or close to nothing, when they feel dry, empty, distracted, and without any delight. It would be difficult to exaggerate the strength of these two convictions.

Yet years in the experience of giving spiritual direction to many sincere people make plain how badly mistaken these assumptions can be. Delight in prayer can be good and given by God, but not all pleasant feelings derive from him. They are not necessarily signs of progress. On the other hand, dryness and emptiness in prayer may be due to willed mediocrity on our part, and when such is the case, they also are not signs of progress. Quite the contrary.

Signs of deepening prayer

How, then, can we know when we are genuinely growing in our communion with the indwelling Lord? Emotions alone give no sure answer. But the Gospels do, and so do the saints. Jesus himself gave us the sure-fire way to discern authenticity, to know what is genuine and what is not: "From their fruits you will know them" (Mt 7:20). We are growing in meditation and contemplation to the extent that we are advancing in humility, patience, love, purity, and all the virtues. The same idea is supposed in 2 John 6: To love is to live the commandments, to live a life of love. Notice: to love is not necessarily to feel good; it is to do what is right, no matter what our emotions may or may not register.

Truth makes a beautiful whole, resplendent in its harmony. When we live truth, we live all the virtues. Our prayer grows in authenticity, depth, and beauty according as the rest of our life grows in authenticity, depth, and beauty. From their fruits you will know them. We cannot control how we feel, but we can control what we do and do not do. What, then, we ask, are some examples of the signs of growing intimacy with God?

Virtuous living

There is an intercausality between holy living and closeness to God: each one produces the other, and in both directions. To be humble, patient, magnanimous, and zealous is to grow in intimacy with the Lord. In the opposite direction, to be deep in him prompts us to develop in each of these virtues and in all the others as well. Hence,

whether we feel dry and empty at prayer or full of consolation and delight, if the virtues are flourishing, if we
are growing in selfless love and fidelity to our duties of
state, our prayer is growing. There is nothing merely sen-
timental here; these are down-to-earth facts. Authenticity
works.

Generosity in serving others

There is only one virtue of love, and by it we love God,
ourselves, and our neighbors, whether the latter are attractive or not. And love is not love unless it is ready to
serve, to seek another's benefit, even to prefer another's
advantage over our own (Phil 2:4). Much of what the
world considers love is mere attraction or self-centered
lust or ignoble egocentrism: What can I get from you?
"If you salute those who salute you, what good is that?"
asked Jesus (Mt 5:47). The perfect picture of genuine love
is this same Lord on the cross. When we love as he loved
us, we have a deep prayer life (Jn 13:34–35).

Being drawn to a healthy solitude

Some people may think that this sign is incompatible with
serving others. Quite the contrary is the case. Why? As
we have already noted—and in our noisy age it may be
wise to note it again—solitude is not isolation. It is a
time to be alone with the supreme Alone, and this is necessary for our personal growth. Isolation is rejecting others, and this is, of course, damaging to oneself and to others as well. Two people in love, real love, spontaneously

desire, and with good reason, to be alone with each other. They have worthwhile things to share. A person growing in closeness to God increasingly seeks to be alone with him, often in a wordless presence-to-presence.

Love for the Church

St. Augustine (and Vatican Council II, which cited him) made the classical remark that "a person possesses the Holy Spirit to the extent of his love for Christ's Church" (OT, no. 9). Jesus in the New Testament so identifies himself with the Church he founded and loved into being that he is able to say that "he who hears you, hears me, and he who rejects you, rejects me" (Lk 10:16); and "as long as you did it to the least of mine, you did it to me" (Mt 25:40). It has been a striking trait of the saints through the centuries, even into our own day, that men and women of deep prayer, genuine prayer, are outstanding in their love for the Church, the temple of the Holy Spirit on earth.

Embracing factual frugality

You may have already noticed two traits in these signs of growth in prayer depth. One is that they are all christocentric, rooted in the Lord himself. Which is to say that they are divinely originated. The other trait is that they are like pieces in a gorgeous mosaic: they present a splendid picture of what gospel holiness is in every state of life. So also factual frugality. Married saints as well as their clerical and religious brothers and sisters dislike superfluities, what they and their families do not need. One reason for this unusual outlook, so unlike that of worldly people, is that people close to God love other people too, with a self-sacrificing love. Logically enough, they want to share their material goods with those who suffer want. They are happy to give up what does not lead to God (1 Jn 3:17–18; Tit 2:11, JB). These men and women are well aware that in this life we are all only pilgrims, here but for a short time, and our Master had no place to lay his head (1 Pet 2:11; Mt 8:20). As their prayer deepens they progressively discover that the most precious things in life are free of charge. In their supreme Beloved they have everything they need . . . and more.

Attraction to the cross

Yes, this trait also is nonsense to the worldly minded. Suffering with love is another name for this sign of deep prayer. Everyone suffers. Some profit from it, and some do not. The former suffer with love and in union with Jesus being tortured to death for us. The latter are loveless and perhaps bitter, often finding fault with everyone but themselves.

Suffering of itself does not improve a person. If you and I become grouchy or cynical in our hardships, we are getting worse, not better. But if we embrace the pain with willed love, we are growing. By ourselves, of course, we cannot do this. But with the aid of advancing prayer we then have "the strength based on his own glorious power, . . . to bear *anything joyfully*" (Col 1:11, JB, emphasis added). Imagine: anything . . . joyfully! This is a mark of a splendid human being, one being "transformed from one glory to another" into the divine image (2 Cor 3:18). This is part of a real growth in prayer intimacy with purest Joy and Love, the Lord himself.

Absence of self-centeredness

Egocentrism is a clear consequence of original sin. A baby is entirely absorbed in its own tiny being, though with no guilt. Only with slow formation and decades of effort are we gradually freed from selfish focusing on our desires, preferences, and pleasures. Purifying contemplative prayer is an indispensable help in giving up an absorption in ourselves: impatience, laziness, vanities, overindulgences in food and drink, desires to be noticed and praised. Falling more deeply in love as prayer grows prompts us to surrender gladly to the Lord's "conquering delight" (to borrow St. Augustine's expression), a delight that immeasurably surpasses the trivialities of worldliness. And this suggests our final sign of making progress in prayer.

God, focus of habitual attention

Anyone in love needs no prodding to be reminded of the beloved. Where our treasure is, there also our heart will be, as Jesus himself put it (Lk 12:34). St. Paul had a similar thought: since we have risen with Christ, so our minds are to be on the things above, not on those of earth (Col 3:1-3). That is, our minds should be spontaneously centered on the indwelling Trinity. As contemplation deepens, we are less and less drawn to the shallow amusements of the worldly: useless and even harmful television, idle gossip, overindulgent dining and drinking. Having the best, we are disinclined toward the least.

~

A final caution is a forewarning. Even with all our assurances about these genuine marks of valuable prayer and its growth, they are hard to believe and to apply to oneself when the going gets rough. Clear as these signs are, experience shows that they easily fade into oblivion when they are most needed. So distressing are the experiences of dryness and apparent emptiness, especially when they are protracted, that people can scarcely believe that their situation is worthwhile. This chapter, therefore, needs to be read and re-read, over and over—especially later on when it seems that "nothing is happening during the times I give to prayer."

For a fuller discussion of how to evaluate progress, see SSD, chapter 12, pp. 267–78.

18

Growing in Depth

Because contemplation in all its richness is the most living of all our human activities, it normally grows to a fullness. Communing with God is anything but static, dull, and dreary. Because Jesus came that we might have a vibrant life that develops to an overflowing abundance (Jn 10:10), we now in our final chapter touch on deepening our intimacy with the indwelling Trinity, even to the point of being "filled with the utter fullness of God" (Eph 3:19, JB).

We now take for granted all we have said in our previous chapters. For example, "growing in prayer" does not mean adding a multitude of more vocal prayers, though not a few people seem to think it does. We are not to babble as the pagans do (Mt 6:7).

We likewise assume that we have learned how to balance and integrate the provision of ample time for daily meditation/contemplation with work, rest, family, and community duties—neglecting neither the one nor the others. As Vatican Council II put it, we are "eager to act and devoted to contemplation" (SC, no. 2).

We suppose also that our readers understand how meditation and contemplation differ, where they are in their development, and thus how they should be praying, lest they hinder what the Lord is giving to them. We are now ready to reflect on impediments to this growth and then to proceed on to consider the degrees of conversion that go hand in hand with progress toward the summit.

Impediments

First, a basic principle: Our prayer deepens to the extent that our living of the gospel generously deepens. Or, to put the matter in other words, communing with God is authentic if our life-style is authentic. Truth is symphonic. God does not play games. He pays us the compliment of expecting our sincerity. The whole matter is simple. Mortal sin kills divine life, and deliberate venial sin dulls it. We are talking now about acts of free will, not mere inclinations or feelings or temptations (see SSD, pp. 230–33).

Even human love is cooled or killed by egocentric selfishness. So also with divine love. We will suppose at this moment that we are in the state of grace, that we have not chosen an idol incompatible with God. Yet the list of possible impediments to further growth is painfully plain: lack of showing warmth toward an unattractive person, willed showing of impatience, gossiping about others' faults, overeating, laziness, grouchiness, undisciplined use of television, radio, Internet. Deliberate worldliness and a lack of mortifying our tendencies to drift off to petty idols are incompatible with deepening immersion in the indwelling Trinity. To the extent that we want selfishness, to that extent we do not want closeness to our infinitely lovable God. (For details, see SSD, pp. 216–30.)

Degrees of conversion

It follows therefore that to deepen our intimacy with the incomparable Lord of our life, we must imitate the prodigal son in his conversion from a life of sin to a return to his father. This is true of any human love. There can be no genuine and deep relationship if one or both parties are openly offending the other and doing nothing to change their behavior. There are three main degrees in this critical reversal of wayward self-centeredness. (See SSD, p. 260.)

The first conversion is turning away from a serious rejection of God and going back to him, that is, renouncing mortal sin. By that we mean, for example, giving up a willed hatred for another person or avarice or lust or grave injustice. We mean reversing one's rejection of divine revelation and the Church commissioned by Jesus to teach it in his name. There can be no vibrant prayer life when one says No to the divine message and makes no effort to climb out of the quagmire of sin. This is the conversion of the prodigal son. And we know from the sheer beauty of that parable how God loves the repentant sinner (Lk 15:11–32).

The second degree is to give up willed venial sins (mere feelings or temptations are not sins). Though these lesser sins do not alienate a person from God, they do hinder progress. Some of these petty idols we have mentioned above. When this change occurs, meditative, contemplative, and liturgical prayer begins to flourish.

The third and highest degree of conversion is the practice of heroic virtue, that is, living as the saints live: men and women who love without limit. These are the beautiful ones who not only obey all the commandments and avoid all sins, great and small—they go farther. They are people head over heels in love, genuine selfless love. They give fully to God and to others, even when there are no obligations (Ps 119:10; Lk 10:27). They are men and women who are prayerful throughout the day, even while they do not neglect their work or other people. They rejoice and thank God even in bitter deprivations and other sufferings (Col 1:11, 24; Heb 10:34). They are converted to an entire holiness, each one in his own state of life. Whether they be married or priests or religious, they are a new creation living a spiritual revolution (2 Cor 5:17; Eph 4:22–24). They cut no corners. Not surprisingly, their prayer wonderfully deepens. (See CCC 2725; FW, pp. 26–30, 184–85, 199; SSD, p. 158.)

Hints for growth

It becomes clear, therefore, that growing in divine intimacy is not automatic, not simply a matter of getting on in years with no significant changes in how we live day by day. We need not here repeat what we have said elsewhere in much detail. See SSD, pp. 247–66, where we have shared no less than forty-four hints on making progress in the spiritual life. If we put these suggestions into practice, we shall soon be saints. They are effective, but not because I have written them. They simply make the gospel concrete and specific. Our immediate purpose is modest: just a few more reflections to supplement those hints.

1. We need to keep our eyes wide open to avoid the gradual slide into mediocrity. Many young people on the day of marriage or ordination or religious profession are determined to go all the way with God, but only too often, eight or ten or fifteen years later, not a few of them have gradually and imperceptibly become luke-warm. They are no longer on fire. They may make annual retreats, and resolve to improve after each one of them, but a month or two later the resolutions have vaporized away. They are back into the rut of mediocrity. The question to ask is: What must *I* do to remain determined? No one else can do it for me.

2. In our last chapter we spoke of attraction to the cross as a sign of progress in prayer. We now add that it is a condition of growing further in depth of communion with the Lord. We cannot be disciples unless we carry our cross with him in his crucifixion (Lk 9:23). If we die with him, we shall rise with him (Rom 6:3–5; Jn 12:24). Attraction to the cross does not mean that we have a natural liking for it but that with our free will we do basically two things. One is to accept the sufferings that come our way in union with Jesus in his passion. Yes, we do what we reasonably can to correct what is amiss in our world, but we also generously embrace with love the many hardships in life that cannot be avoided. The second basic here is that we actively take on the sacrifices en-tailed in getting rid of our faults: laziness, overeating, idle

gossiping, salacious entertainments, wasting time with useless television, disciplining impatience. Immense benefits for prayer accompany people who live in these ways. "For those who love God everything works together for the good" (Rom 8:28; see also FW, pp. 126–27).

3. Our third hint for growing is to live fully in the present moment: seize it right now; profit from it; live this minute and this hour. Wherever you may be on the path toward God, however little you might be today, if you respond to this truth, this goodness, this beauty here in front of you, you are farther along on the way. If at the table I look at an orange or a cherry with real appreciation, pausing to note its unique splendor, I become a better person. They are works of art meant to nourish our minds and hearts as well as to feed our bodies. Absorbing the beautiful (and therefore, most of all, supreme Beauty) is an admonition we have in Scripture itself: the inspired word invites us to come and ponder the marvels of the Lord, the astonishing things he has done in our world (Ps 46:8). Because we do not do this automatically, we ask him to open the eyes of our minds that we may focus on and admire his words and deeds (Ps 119:18, 27). If we acquire this habit, we are on the way to deeper conversion, deeper prayer. You might consider again chapter 5, "Elegant variety". As a matter of fact, since we tend to forget most of what we read, returning to all of our chapters may well be in order.

4. Our final reflection is that we make a point of keeping before our mind's eye the conviction that God is, and shall remain, number one on our list of priorities. When he is our "one thing", we then love ourselves and

our dear ones all the more realistically, purely, deeply—
through thick and thin. As St. Augustine put it so suc-
cinctly in seven syllables: "To pray well one must live
well." When this happens we shall indeed then "be filled
with the utter fullness of God" (Eph 3:19, JB).

INDEX